MW01688896

BOOTH

BUTLER UNIVERSITY

COVER ART

Fillmore by Kevin Cyr

LAYOUT & PAGE DESIGN

Katie Orlowski and
Print Marketing & Communications,
Butler University

We publish new material every week on our website, as well as two print issues a year. We accept electronic submissions only from September to April 15 at *booth.submittable.com/submit*. Full guidelines on website. We are grateful for the ongoing support of the Butler University MFA program and the College of Liberal Arts & Sciences at Butler University.

VISIT OUR WEBSITE

booth.butler.edu

Contents

Contents

Three Larissa Stories

Teresa Milbrodt

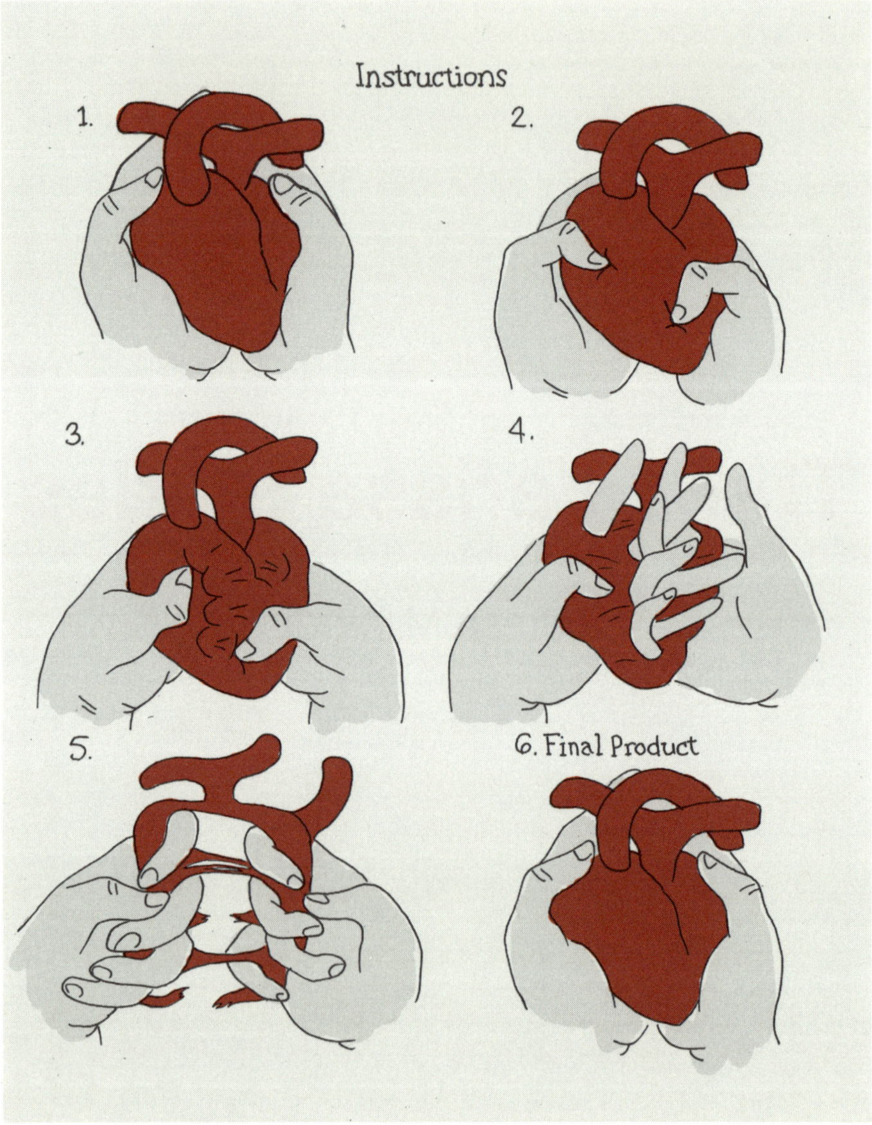
Instructions
1.
2.
3.
4.
5.
6. Final Product

Larissa and Elementary Chemistry

Teresa Milbrodt

This was when we were ten and eight: My sister and I fed our white mouse fireflies until it started glowing like a lightbulb about to go out, but you couldn't see it unless you turned off the lamp or covered the mouse's cage with a blanket and stuck your head underneath, and we didn't do that a lot because it smelled bad. At night we let the mouse run around our bedroom floor and scare the cat so it hid under the bed, but the mouse was smart and didn't follow. We thought she was a mouse like an angel, like the ghost of all mice that had died when they were eaten by eagles and foxes and cats, or mice that died in traps our dad set in the garage. He said those were bad mice that carried diseases, they weren't like our white mouse, but it was sad and gross and I still hate destroying furry life, even small smelly disease-carrying furry life that eats my cat's food and leaves pellets in the pantry.

But when I was ten all of nature was bright and shining and on July nights my sister and I ran around the backyard, going after fireflies as the mosquitoes went after us, but we didn't feel their needle noses because we were cramming glowbugs into our peanut-butter jar. We never put holes in the lid because we wanted the insects dead by morning since our mouse ate fireflies like candy, only wanted those crunchy bulbs.

We got a second mouse (the guy at the pet shop who had pimples like constellations said it was a boy) and fed it fireflies, too, until both mice glowed like nightlights, only they weren't bright enough to read by even when we put them on a book. At two in the morning we woke up and heard the mice skittering in the cedar shavings, and after that our second mouse started to inflate like a little white balloon, and it turned out she wasn't a boy, and that was when I learned never to believe people who work in pet shops. Somehow the babies glowed, but we didn't know why because they hadn't eaten fireflies.

"Somehow the babies glowed, but we didn't know why because they hadn't eaten fireflies."

Then this awful thing happened and the father ate one of those babies and we were so mad we wanted to squeeze him to death, but our mom said we couldn't be too mad at the father mouse because it was instinct and we had to understand that. We didn't understand that nature meant eating your babies, but we didn't kill him since neither of us wanted to be the one to do it.

After a week we put him back in the big mouse cage because we wanted the mice to make up and be a family, and he went after those babies because he still hadn't learned, and my sister screamed and grabbed him too tight. We didn't hear anything, but a little red drop of blood came out of the mouse's mouth. That was it.

We tried to give the mouse to the cat but she wouldn't eat it, so we wrapped him in toilet paper and troweled a grave in the flower bed. At night we looked on the floor for his guilty glowing ghost, but never saw anything.

My sister whispered to me in the dark that she didn't mean to do it, and I said I knew that, and for the moment that made everything okay. We still had seven baby mice that crowded around their mother to nurse, and when we let them run around on the rug they left little glowing pellets like stardust. Before bed we dared each other to eat just one firefly and see if in the morning our little toe, perhaps the tip of a finger, would glow with that strange and tiny light, but we always backed out and said maybe tomorrow. Now I wish I would have done it, because it was still a time when anything might have happened.

Larissa Goes into Business

Teresa Milbrodt

You can't blame me because we were in second grade, the economy was based on lunchtime desserts, and I never had anything good. That's why I sold my boyfriend, Chris, to Jenny for two chocolate cream-filled cupcakes. Chris had refused to marry me and wouldn't even kiss me on the playground behind the slide. As part of the deal, I had to take Jenny's boyfriend, Mark, and everyone knew Mark picked his nose and ate it. I made Mark bring me a candy bar every time he kissed me on the cheek, and I told him he had to kiss me because that's what girlfriends and boyfriends did. I didn't breathe when his lips touched my skin so I wouldn't sniff the boogers on his breath.

By the end of the week all the girls in second grade had realized my brilliance and claimed a boyfriend, except for poor Kate who had to take Doug since no one else wanted him. Doug lived with his grandparents who were from some country that no one could pronounce. He wore glasses and smelled funny, like the weird rice and vegetable mixtures his grandmother packed in his lunch. Everyone knew it was stuff she picked out of the garbage disposal and threw into a bowl.

But Doug brought Kate a bracelet on the Wednesday after he had been declared her boyfriend. It was the fake-gold-chain kind with shiny paint that wore off in a few weeks, but it was better than a candy bar. We clustered around Kate to examine the present. On Friday Doug gave her a little sampler box of chocolates, and Kate kissed him on the cheek without Doug even having to ask. He and Kate held hands as they waited in the bus line to go home.

Doug's value skyrocketed. Kate was offered candy, dolls, one week of lunch desserts, even Eric, the most popular boy in class, in trade for Doug. She refused. I was sick of Mark, so I convinced Hillary that Mark was a great boyfriend because he brought you all the candy you wanted and he didn't smell that much like boogers. Hillary agreed to trade me her boyfriend, Nick, if I threw in some gumdrops. I sighed but gave her the gumdrops because Nick's mother made the best chocolate-chip cookies of any mother in the second grade. Then I had a "talk" with Nick by the slide at recess and quietly explained that if he didn't bring me at least four cookies the next day I'd trade him to Mallory. Everyone knew Mallory still wet the bed.

"Hillary agreed to trade me her boyfriend, Nick, if I threw in some gumdrops."

Some of the boys didn't care whose boyfriend they were. They were assured of their value because they were cute or athletic and in no danger of getting stuck with a bed-wetting Mallory in the near future, or even having to surrender half of their dessert. But other boys, those who hung their coats on the lower racks in the back of the classroom, realized that there was status to be gained through being paired with the right girl, and status to be lost through being attached to Mallory.

After Nick brought me cookies, I told my best friend, Trish, what I'd said to him. Soon she was dragging her boyfriend, Aaron, away from his soccer game and to the slide for a "little talk." Aaron just drank milk at lunch the next day and told the cafeteria lady he wasn't hungry, but after school in the bus line, Trish showed us girls her four packs of gum.

The next day we heard that Chris was grounded for a month because he'd tried to steal two bags of red licorice from the drugstore across the street from school. They were for Jenny, but because he didn't have them, Jenny traded him to Mallory. Chris escaped lunchtime in the cafeteria, and Trish whispered to me that he locked himself in a bathroom stall to eat his sandwich and pretzels. He was scared that someone would make him kiss Mallory on the playground at recess.

Rumor had it that Aaron and Sean were working together to lift candy bars and gum from the gas station across the street—one kid distracted the cashier with questions while the other kid slipped candy into his backpack—but this was not our concern. This was second grade, and the law of the jungle prevailed. Pretty soon Aaron and Sean topped the social ladder along with Doug, even though they all had glasses and everyone knew their mothers sent notes in their lunch sacks.

We never found out who squealed to the teacher. Probably Chris. We got a half-hour talk on how trade was mean, and after that the lunch and recess monitors watched us like prison guards. There could be no more exchange of cookies or candy or jewelry until later, years later, when we were wearing lipstick and mascara, short skirts and high heels. Now the trade meant bras and back seats, dinners and diamonds. Now the competition was serious. But we already knew the rules of the game.

Larissa's Greatest Fear

Teresa Milbrodt

I'm making breakfast, oatmeal with lots of raisins and brown sugar and cinnamon and chocolate chips, because I don't want it to taste healthy but I'm at the age when I have to worry about my colon and pacify it with fiber and direct kind thoughts toward it. I feel this pain in my right side and stop with my spoon in the air and the microwave still running. I have to watch the oatmeal so it doesn't explode out of the bowl, but I worry the pain is a harbinger of doom, the first sign of appendicitis. My dad had it when he was a kid and said it felt like he had the flu, then he threw up, then he had a stabbing knife cramp in his right side and had to go to the emergency room.

This is my nightmare, the stomachache that gets worse and then I have to be cut open before something explodes, and my oatmeal is done, it has exploded all over the microwave like my appendix will do someday because it's out to get me. The appendix is an organ scientists say humans used to need but don't anymore, so I wonder why it wasn't phased out like rotary phones or milkmen or chalkboards that use real chalk. We have better organs, new and improved, so there's nothing for the appendix to do but get bored and inflamed. I make new oatmeal because my colon needs me and my colon is something I still need, unlike my appendix, but I can't eat because there's that pain in my right side.

On my walk to my new job at the shoe store I consider how tiny and innocuous things sometimes aren't, how scissors and sticks take out eyes and certain bees are evil and you can get hit by lightning when the sky is blue.

"The appendix is an organ scientists say humans used to need but don't anymore, so I wonder why it wasn't phased out like rotary phones . . ."

Millions of these warnings scroll under the screen on the nightly news, which makes me wonder how the hell anyone is still alive when the latest bulletin is about this guy in Memphis who fell off a ladder and got knocked unconscious and drowned in four inches of water. My stomach is unhappy because it is empty and I can hear my appendix muttering but I can't make out the words. I tell the guy who's outside the shoe store with a coffee cup full of change that my appendix is talking to me, and he asks if I need a quarter to call someone, but I can't call my appendix so I shake my head and think about the number of people who are killed by vending machines every year. I know I saw the statistic somewhere and it was higher than I expected but there was no explanation of how it happened, if the victims aggravated the vending machines or if they were just maneuvering the machine to coax out their bag of chips, a small thing that did not seem dangerous.

New York Times Best Sellers

Scott William Woods

SUNDAY, JANUARY 4, 2015

Combined Book and Print Book Best Sellers

THIS WEEK	LAST WEEK	FICTION	WEEKS ON LIST
1		**CROSS EYED**, by James Patterson. (Little, Brown & Company.) Only District of Columbia detective-psychologist Alex Cross can avert a constitutional crisis when the vice president is accused of murdering the president.	1
2		**INCA RUINS**, by James Patterson and Grant Blackwood. (Patterson, Little, Brown.) An ancient evil catapults Alex Cross into a catastrophic series of space-time-identity aberrants.	1
3	1	**A BRACE OF SPELLS**, by James Patterson and George R. R. Martin. (Patterson Fantasy.) Thrust through a wormhole, a detective joins a young swordsman to confront the darkness.	2
4		**PLAINSMAN**, by James Patterson and Larry McMurtry. (James Patterson University Press.) Call and McCrae get unexpected help on the trail of a former Texas Ranger turned serial killer.	1
5		**CROSS MY HEART**, by James Patterson and Nora Roberts. (Patterson-Harlequin-Silhouette.) A feisty young woman struggles to deny her hopeless love for Alex Cross.	1
6		**FORESAKEN**, by James Patterson and Francine Rivers. (Patterson Christian Publishing.) A psychologist counsels a minister through her crisis of faith, with help from his Nana Mama.	1
7		**FIFTY SHADES OF CROSS**, by James Patterson and E. L. James. (Patterson Vintage.) The detective explores his neglected sadomasochistic erotic side, with help from his Nana Mama.	1
8		**SHE**, by James Patterson and Stephen King. (Patterson Scribner.) In a small town in Maine, an imp transforms a troubled teenaged girl into an unwitting serial killer.	1

9		**HUNGER CROSS**, by James Patterson and Suzanne Collins. (Patterson Scholastic Books.) "Coaxed" into the future, a D.C. homicide cop competes for his life against a serial killer.	1
10		**INTERPRETER OF ALEX**, by James Patterson and Jhumpa Lahiri. (Patterson Publishers.) A tightly knit multigenerational community of Indian immigrants is targeted by a serial killer.	1
11	2	**MIDDLECROSS**, by James Patterson and Jeffrey Eugenides. (Patterson House.) The bite of a hervamphropire renders Alex Cross intersexual and precipitates a sextangle with a straight man, a straight woman, a gay man, a lesbian, and a serial killer.	3
12	3	**THE GIRL WITH THE DRAGON CROSS**, by James Patterson and Stieg Larsson. (Patterson Acquired Copyrights.) Temporarily suspended for libel, Alex Cross teams with a hacker to investigate the disappearance of a girl 36 years ago in Sweden.	3
13	4	**GONE WITH THE WIND**, by James Patterson and Margaret Mitchell. (Patterson Amazon & Noble.) The classic tale, as retold by Alex Cross, great-great-grandfather of Alex Cross.	5
14	5	**JP**, by James Patterson, John Grisham, and Dan Brown. (James Patterson.) Despite humble origins, a young man grows to author or coauthor 90 percent of all hardcover fiction sales, through determination, respect for others, and a firm belief in himself and serial killers.	2
15		**BEING JAMES PATTERSON**, by Arnold West. (Random House.) An average Joe becomes entrapped in the brain of a popular author.	1

Thirteen Ways of Looking at New York

Micah Ling and Douglas Light

1.
Water, then water, then water. Then
Sudden runway. LGA summer '95.
My trip, specific: 10 days. Heat
And a woman await.
Round trip tickets only work
If you make the return.

2.
Just before Christmas, transit is on strike.
You say, *Tell the driver you won't pay a dollar*
more than twenty; take down their number.
I do, and get out early, in traffic, to walk
the rest of the way, on the spine of your street.

3.
Twice I saw her
naked. Winter. The air sparked with
hope and confusion. On the stoop
3rd Street. Out front of Quentin Crisp's
Got a cigarette? she'd ask
every day, clothed or not. Hungry

or not. Ranting
or not. People mistake love for a noun.
I'd have handed her a life's worth
had I had any. Smoke
was the least of her worries.

4.
From Montana to Yankee Stadium: the Bronx,
and it all smelled just right.
Peanut shells, draught, a different kind of fresh
that held everything from the radio.

5.
He grasps my arm, holds me still.
Crying men are a sadness difficult to endure.
My wife. My girlfriend. My girlfriend-wife, he says,
terrified by a truth he can't uncreate.

"Turkey in the Straw" tears
the February air. Mister Softee, selling treats
other than ice cream, is long

gone when the police arrive.

6.

Earlier this week, at a gas station in Tennessee
I was mistaken for a boy: told, *That's the women's*
restroom. I nodded, laughed, like tripping
on a curb in front of a crowd. But today,
here, in this Brooklyn apartment,
you've got me down to my panties
and feeling more like a woman than ever before.

7.

We sat outside drinking warm, flat soda
watching people trundle south
only south
toward the bridges tethering Brooklyn
toward what the world watched

For two weeks, more
ID was required to access
streets south of 14th

I had to prove a right to be here
prove I somehow belonged.

8.

My only friends are songs: anthems to greatness,
and a few winding roads. I'm thinking this when you call
from the city: there on business. You're not speaking

in complete sentences, but I know you need help:
my help. Hundreds of miles away, all I can do is nod
to the beat of a song, and hope that you hear it.

9.
Eating crabs on the F trains
she gnawed at legs
the shell, spitting shards to the
floor.

A hundred and thirty-six thousand
I earned that year and drank the stress
clean each night. Fear of failing
never washed away.

With her mouth brined with bits,
crablady stood, hiked
her skirt and announced
Truly, I'm sorry.

Her urine forged the path
of least resistance when we
lurched to a stop
at West 4th.

10.
Do you know how long it lasts
when you say, *Only you*
would appreciate how
exquisitely I cross Lexington
Avenue, on my walk from the subway
to the Met? It lasts forever, and I can smell
the flower shop on 85th
because it reminds you of Camp Otterbein:
where we're grass-stained and grinning.

11.
Morning, Westside Highway,
traffic tight, gleaming. 70 mph. Right
the hard Hudson. Left
the blurring wall.

When we speak of strength
we speak of the physical. Hold
the motorcycle firm, keep it from coming apart.
Don't caress what can't be returned.

But the Hudson is blurring! The wall is hard!
The traffic gleaming, beautiful, tight!

There is another strength
one we don't speak of.

12.
The first time I stood in Times Square, I was a child:
maybe six years old. And it was better
than Disney World. Pouring rain, and all I wanted
was for the man with the black umbrella to let me
hail the cab: let me get my little arm out there
and start living the life of being noticed.

13.
It's a mild autumn and everything smells warm:
New York is where the light stops being light,
just on the edge of deep color. I stop:
it starts being something else. I've lived

for an afternoon coffee: little buzz, little wink,
elsewhere, the cul-de-sacs of the heart.
Then, someone steals my eye: my whole body.
Here, I'm forced left. I'm forced right.

Prince, Purple Rain

Micah Ling

I'm the daughter of a preacher man, which is to say, I was born to be bad.
I worship motorcycles to no end. Once, I had a man record revving
his engine, his beautiful bike, and leave it for me, as a voicemail.
And yes, I was thinking more about the man than the pipes, but, just
barely.

I worship motorcycles to no end, and I listened to that revving
over and over: it made my heart beat faster, like hearing
dirty things from the man with the pipes, just barely
audible—the kinds of secrets that can turn ears red—hot.

Over and over, when my heart beats faster, I remember hearing
(the first time), him say it was so good, that it felt so good
out loud—all of it made his ears turn red—hot:
sweating—really dripping—like I didn't know people could sweat.

The first time—he said it was so good: felt so good
of course. But what I never told him, have still never told him
through the sweating—the dripping—more than I knew people could,
was that I was trying to be younger and older at once.

Of course—we all are—but what I didn't tell him: never told him
was that it was all a dream: some sort of myth or made-up memory
the two of us trying to be younger and older at once
until we stopped: we breathed. Then the smells and tastes were real, finally.

Now it isn't a dream or a myth or a made-up memory:
I'm the daughter of a preacher man, which is to say, I was born to be bad
until I stop: I breathe. And the smells, the tastes, are real, finally,
as real as an engine—a beautiful bike—as real as a voice, left for me.

I
KNOW
it
HURTS

A Conversation with Chuck Klosterman

Chris Speckman

Chuck Klosterman is a pop-culture savant who talks sports for Grantland *and dispenses advice in his Ethicist column for* The New York Times Magazine. *Along the ride, he's also written for* Spin, Esquire, GQ, The Believer, *and* The Washington Post. *Klosterman is perhaps best known for his five books of non-fiction and essays*—Fargo Rock City*;* Sex, Drugs, and Cocoa Puffs*;* Killing Yourself to Live*;* Chuck Klosterman IV*; and* Eating the Dinosaur—*and a pair of novels,* Downtown Owl *and* The Visible Man.

In January, Klosterman visited Butler University to read from his new collection of essays, I Wear The Black Hat: Grappling with Villains (Real and Imagined), *for the first time. Before he stepped foot in Indy, Klosterman chatted with* Booth *contributing editor Chris Speckman on the phone about the falsification of memory, the beauty of Jimi Hendrix's mistakes, the similarities between* The Wire *and Russian literature, the idea of Dave Eggers, a legendary junior-college basketball game in North Dakota, and the dream of not hating something you've written a decade after its publication.*

How old were you when you began to have aspirations of being a writer? What initially drew you to reading and writing when you were younger?

When I was a kid in elementary and middle school, I was maybe more interested in writing and reading than other kids, although not to the point where I thought, *This is what I want to do for a living.* That's not because I had some sort of apprehension or distaste or insecurity—I just didn't think of writing as a way to make a living.

I was pretty old before it occurred to me that it was a viable career. When I went to college at the University of North Dakota, I assumed that I would probably become an English teacher and a football coach or a basketball coach. Not because I had this dream of doing that, but it just seemed like something I would be good at. Then I found out that our college newspaper paid people to work at it, and it blew my mind. I figured that was way better than getting a standard job. I started writing for the newspaper, and it was just a natural thing. I felt like I was okay at it right from the get-go. I started working as an editor, and I just loved it. It was so fun. I loved the people I worked with. I realized that if I majored in journalism, at least I knew what the job was at the end. At that time, I sort of thought that working at a newspaper would be my life. I still wasn't really thinking of book writing necessarily. Eventually, I just tried to see if I could do it. I was working in Ohio, and I wanted to see if I could write a book-length manuscript.

"There are some people who seem like they would write even if no one was going to see their work. They have the need to prove it to themselves that this worldview exists. I'm not like that."

So it was never like I had this dream, and the dream was fulfilled. It was like I fell into the dream that I did not know I was having.

I've heard you talk about people who have to write—people who just have that compulsion. Would you say that you're someone like that or more like someone who has simply found a career as a writer that's preferable to any alternative?

I do love writing. But I don't feel a compulsion to write the way some writers suggest. There isn't a great separation for me between thinking about something and writing about something. Writing about something is almost the process of working through my thoughts on it. I don't write anything that isn't published. To me, that's the difference. There are some people who seem like they would write even if no one was going to see their work. They have the need to prove it to themselves that this worldview exists. I'm not like that. If I'm not going to write about something, I'll just think about it. I don't need to share it with other people. However, I think sharing it with people is a great way to live. The process of writing is always pleasant. Maybe not always pleasant, but always engaging. The process of publishing is often not. Sometimes I hate the process of publishing. But you have to publish in order to keep writing. That's just the way it works.

So you've never been a person who keeps a diary or writes secret poetry or jots down lots of notes about things that are going on in your life?

Never.

But it does seem to me that you've managed to catalog a great deal of stuff that has happened to you, and it seems like these may be things that have come out later in your writing. Do you write down a lot of observations, or do you just have a really great memory?

Probably the latter. I think the difference between nonfiction writers—particularly essayists and memoirists—and other people is that they can't really get over the past the way that other people do. I think that's part of my problem. The things that happened to me when I was fifteen or twenty or twenty-five, I still think about, and it feels like I think of them in a very vivid, clear way. That might be a product of my falsification of my memory. Perhaps I remember things, and I'm really just talking about the way I want to remember things, then I create this memory by writing it.

In many ways, it seems like growing up in small-town North Dakota may have limited your exposure to pop culture growing up, at least when compared to the access that a kid who grew up in a place like New York City might have had. Do you think this contributed to your obsession with pop culture that has dominated much of your writing?

I think in a weird way it was definitely an advantage. If you're exposed to a thousand different bands, the process is really just wading through all that material, trying to deduce what has value and what does not. It's almost just like sort of ranking it, and then you need other people to guide you. You need the critics to tell you that bands like the Velvet Underground are important. But when you only have, say, fifty bands, you're as interested in those fifty as you would be the thousand. The amount of time and engagement you have with this small sample size is the same as if you had a huge sample size. You end up thinking about these things with probably a little more intensity.

When I was growing up, Guns N' Roses was the most interesting art in my life. I didn't have access to more interesting films. I could get books, but with those I needed to be a little bit older to be guided along. So I would think about Guns N' Roses the way I probably would have thought about something conventional high art if I had grown up in Manhattan.

Do you think your background in journalism and looking through other people's eyes sparked your interest in the kind of voyeurism that is the cornerstone of The Visible Man*? Or do you think your natural interest in others led you to pursue journalism?*

That's a very good question. I suppose maybe the former. I hate to say this is a problem, but I have one particular hurdle that is not specific to me only but specific to people like me—because I've done so much first-person essay writing, the assumption is that when I write anything, I'm writing about myself. So when I was deciding to start that novel, my initial idea was that I'd need a situation where the Invisible Man character talks about his life to someone directly. The obvious person would be a journalist. But I knew if I did that, everyone would assume the journalist was a stand-in for me. I just knew that would happen, so I thought to myself, *What's another situation where someone's able to lecture another person about their life?* A therapist is the other option. In a way it's even more limitless because there's the assumption that the therapist will tell no one.

So what's really happening in that book is just one really long interview. So it is in a way journalistic. If somebody said "What is *The Visible Man* about?" the obvious answer is that it's about the reality of being by yourself. But there's also a lot about the idea of interviewing and the problems of interview, but also the fact that, despite its flaws, there's no better way to understand other people than asking them direct questions.

So you would say that the repetition of interviewing people led you to see that?

Totally. But the biggest thing is that from 1991 until 2001, I was pretty much strictly a journalist, and I interviewed probably a thousand people in various ways, sometimes for big profiles, sometimes for ten minutes because I'm doing some bullshit story on a zoning law. So I'm doing interviews for ten years, and then these books come out, and all of the sudden, I was being interviewed more than I was actually interviewing. Definitely between 2005 and 2006, I was being interviewed way more often than I was interviewing people. That changed my perspective, too. I know I'm not the only person who this has happened to. But I do think that I have a relatively unique perspective on the process of interviewing because I've done so much of both sides of it.

In The Visible Man, *the character Y— asserts that the difference between fiction and nonfiction is that "only fictional stories require an explanation. Only fictional stories can't have accidents." Is this a belief that you also buy into, and, if so, have you found the process of writing novels to be more challenging and taxing than writing essays and nonfiction?*

> "I would say on a difficulty scale of one to ten, journalism is maybe a two, writing an essay is a four, and writing fiction is probably a nine."

The answer to the second part is absolutely. It's much harder. I would say on a difficulty scale of one to ten, journalism is maybe a two, writing an essay is a four, and writing fiction is probably a nine.

And this is why. So you're doing this interview with me right now, and what would be the best thing that could happen from your perspective? It would be if I said something that made no fucking sense whatsoever, if I said something that was just crazy and a total non sequitur. Or if I was talking to you and said, "Oh, I'm looking out my window right now, and I'm seeing a murder happen." That would be great for your story, because in nonfiction, what you're looking for are things that make no sense. Those are the moments of tension in a nonfiction piece, when a subject says something unexpected or an event happens that's just a huge coincidence. But in fiction, people hate that. People are always looking for the reality of a fake world that accurately reflects their world. So you're constantly looking at these problems and saying, *What is the most reasonable thing that could happen here? What could happen here that would make somebody say, "I could totally see that happening."*

It's an interesting limitation, and it gets even harder for people who write movies and television. Take a show like *Homeland* for example. If people have issues with *Homeland*, it's always about the verisimilitude. Did something happen in this show that doesn't seem real to them? The whole thing is based off making it seem boring enough that it could happen in real life.

I've heard you mention in interviews that writers should first be comfortable with their own work and not worry so much about their audience. Yet, I found there are several very "meta" passages in The Visible Man, *where concerns of the audience seem to be directly addressed, like how Victoria classifies Y—'s long-winded narratives as "astounding to the point of pretension" and how Y— points out his good fortune in finding the exact tools he needs to quickly drug Valerie. Was this meta-ness brought into the book by editors, or an impulse inside of you?*

If people don't like my writing, one of the things that they don't like about it is that it's too self-aware. I understand that criticism because I have felt that of other people's work. But as a writer, to me, self-awareness is what I equate with thoughtfulness. It's an understanding of your own reality. So I write a book the way I would read it as a critic, which is not perfect. It would be ideal if I could separate those things out and not think of any of it. But the fact of the matter is I've been doing it like this for twenty fucking years. That's how I'm going to be. I can't read anything without sort of perceiving it the way I would as if I was reviewing it.

In your first novel, Downtown Owl, *I was impressed with your almost godlike, encyclopedic knowledge of each character's past, present, and future. Was this a chance for you to catalog some of the more interesting real-life character quirks that you had been exposed to over the years, or was this simply an opportunity to let your imagination run wild?*

I think the best way to describe it would be like this. When I went to college, I met all of these people from towns similar to mine. There are five hundred people in my hometown. I was good friends with a guy at college from a town of seven hundred and fifty people and with a whole bunch of people from a town called Langdon that had three thousand people. We would talk about our memories, and I was shocked by how similar they were—the same kind of people seemed to exist in all these towns. So the people in that book, especially some of the more minor characters, are basically composite sketches of archetypes of people who live in small towns. The details about their lives, I guess I did make up, but I made them up in a way like, *Well, I know this story about Person X. What's a story like that?* I didn't want people to read this book and see themselves in it. But they still did. That's the problem.

When you write a nonfiction book, like I did with *Killing Yourself to Live*, you include people you know. People read that, and they know it's real, but their reaction is *That's not me. That's kind of like me, but not really.* However, if you write a fiction book with characters that aren't real, people are certain they're in it. Everybody I grew up with who I've talked about *Downtown Owl* with assumes they are in the book. It's really interesting.

Even though they have similar elements, I found Downtown Owl *and* The Visible Man *to be very different books. Was there anything you learned from the writing and publishing of the first novel that altered the way you approached the second?*

The first novel, I was just so worried that I was going to fail. And I thought that I was going to fail in a way that was not only disappointing, but humiliating. I'd published four nonfiction books, and certainly *Sex, Drugs, and Cocoa Puffs* was extremely popular. So I knew that if I wrote a novel, it would be published. I knew they would do it even if it was bad. And I had this fear that they wouldn't tell me if it was bad—maybe they wouldn't even be sure. I thought it would be terrible and that the only person who wouldn't know would be me. So then when it came out and people were like, *It's okay. It's fine, I guess,* I was super-relieved. Getting mixed reviews, to me, was the same as getting positive reviews.

"To me, all my books are one book. I'm writing one very, very long book through many different contexts."

When I got to *The Visible Man*, I had much more confidence. I knew I could do it. So I wrote it much faster. It took me probably two and a half years to write *Downtown Owl*. It was a slow process. *The Visible Man*, I finished in eight months. I knew what I wanted to do, and I could just execute it then.

I've heard you say that you get no pleasure in rewriting, and you've already told me that you always write assuming that people will read it. I know some of the time people who write a novel end up having to throw away a lot of their material. Is that something you've had to do?

The honest answer is that I probably should do that, but I really just don't do it that way. I'm hesitant that someone will read this and use it as advice because it's probably bad advice. But when I was very young I read an old interview with Jimi Hendrix. Someone was talking to Jimi Hendrix about the mistakes that he makes on certain records, and he said something along the lines of, "You know, the records are all me, even the mistakes." When I was young, that seemed really meaningful to me. And I still sort of think that way.

If I worked on *The Visible Man* for five years, would it be better? Totally. Absolutely. It would be longer. Who knows what else would be in there. It might have more characters. But that's not how I like to work. I would rather put out a book every other year than four books of a technically higher quality over a twenty-year span. To me, all my books are one book. I'm writing one very, very long book through many different contexts.

Do you feel like you've evolved as a writer over the course of your career?

In good ways and in bad ways. I absolutely feel like I am a much better writer now than I was when I wrote *Fargo Rock City* and *Sex, Drugs, and Cocoa Puffs*. Those books to me seem very poorly written when I read them. They seem kind of under-edited, too conversational, too much reliance on swear words for effect—things I don't like now. That said, I know—and I think this is true for many writers and musicians and filmmakers—that the ideas in those books are in many ways superior to any idea I'll have now, even though I'm way smarter. The ideas in *Fargo Rock City* and *Sex, Drugs, and Cocoa Puffs* were truly my own. They were not filtered through other sources. It was creative in a literal sense. Now, the ideal situation would be if I could have that sort of approach to the world with the writing ability I have now. But that's impossible. That's not how it works.

With the book I just finished, I certainly think it's the best writing structurally I've ever done in my life. There are fewer contradictions in it. The thoughts are clearer. The word choice is better. The more writing you do, the better you get. Although I do have to say, I think this book would have been a much more exciting thing to read if I had written it when I was twenty-five. Going to New York has helped me to become a smarter person. But I have to a degree lost the singularity of the way I saw the world.

Going back to The Visible Man, *I found a few of Y—'s insights to be very powerful and thought-provoking, especially his theory about being guilty vs. feeling the sensation of guilt and how these outcomes are dependent on objective and subjective realities. You seem to come up with a lot of theories to help explain the nature of the world. Do you feel it is important to share these deep, philosophical thoughts, and is it at all a goal of yours to affect the way other people think?*

I wouldn't say it's my goal to impact the way other people think. Even when I would review records or films, it was never my goal to make people see a movie or stop people from buying a record. I'm not really like that. I'm just interested in the experience of being alive. Honestly, I feel like the amount that we're affected by the media is actually more profound than we're willing to admit because it would almost entail us conceding that we've lost the ability to have original thoughts. And I think this is a really important thing. So I guess I'm trying to work out how I feel about it. I want it to be interesting. I want someone to read my book and say, "Well, that's an interesting thing to think about. I don't know if it's necessarily true, but it doesn't seem like a terrible argument, and I was interested in it while I was reading."

I've read that you're not into reading novels partly because you end up judging them based on how you perceive the author's ability to stack up against your own. But has there been anything you've read recently that you've thought was brilliant or required reading?

I actually just read this kind of amazing book. It's a Norwegian novel called *My Struggle*. Now obviously, I don't read a lot of Norwegian novels. I'm not even sure what prompted me. I heard a few people talking about it. The author basically did an eight-book telling of his life, and it was super-controversial because he writes extremely intimate details about family and about himself and about his own inner world as a writer. I would say that was one of the best books about the experience of being writer I've ever read. I don't read a lot of books from other countries, but occasionally I do. The difference is in the way they construct ideas and the way they tell stories. It's jarring enough that it maybe becomes extra engaging. It's kind of like if you only listen to rock music and then all of the sudden you put on a jazz record or a country record—there's a different kind of immediacy. Your ears aren't used to something that's the same, yet different. That was the last great novel I read.

"The way I think about stories is no different than the way someone did in the fifteenth century."

So I'm curious as to where you took your cues from then for the novels that you've written. Were there any authors that you looked up to growing up? Or any great books that maybe served as a template for how to take on something like a novel?

To be totally honest—and again, it sounds like bad advice—but I think to myself *Why do I like nonfiction more than I like fiction?* One reason is that I know nonfiction is real and that it will teach me something even if the book is boring. It's closer to journalism to me. But there's another reason, and it's that most novels are boring. Most novels are written still using the framing devices and narrative structures that date back to the origin of the novel. What's great about it is that it's the one medium that goes back forever. And there's a value in that. But people have changed. Culture has evolved, not necessarily in a good way, but it's changed. The way I think about stories is no different than the way someone did in the fifteenth century.

So when I was writing these novels, all I told myself was *Write this the way you would like to read it, not the way you think books are supposed to be.* And that's a really hard thing to tell yourself. I don't even know what the equivalent would be.

Maybe a self-taught musician?

Maybe. But not exactly. If I met a self-taught piano player, would I hear him play and think to myself, *That's not musical?* It's been ingrained in me how piano music is supposed to sound. So if someone really broke out of that paradigm, I don't know if I would be intellectually prepared for it. But the thing is, I knew that whatever I did wouldn't be that far afield. I know my limitations. I'm not going to write something that was previously unimagined. I'm not like that. Ultimately, I sort of have mainstream tastes in everything.

I sometimes feel the same way about novels, and it seems to me that maybe a lot of people who would be writing great stories in print are now doing it on television. You seem to watch a lot of TV. Do you see critically acclaimed shows like The Wire *and* Breaking Bad *as the new literature and the new structured intellectual backbone of what people are consuming?*

Absolutely, at least from the perspective of the consumer. As far as the actual writing of those shows—I'm not a TV writer, so I don't know how closely that process mirrors literary storytelling. I actually suspect it's probably a little more different than we realize. But from the consuming side, the kind of person who would have been reading a lot of literary fiction in the '70s and now doesn't read any literary fiction, or maybe three novels a year, probably one of them Jonathan Franzen's *Freedom*, they're getting what has replaced that, the high-end television show. For the consumer, watching a show like *Mad Men* really mirrors the experience of reading a well-drawn novel. There's a large narrative. But what you're really looking at is the mini-narratives each character is experiencing throughout the life of the show, which is the exact same feeling. It's similar with *The Wire*. If you were to describe *The Wire* to somebody else, but you couldn't say it's a TV show and you just had to describe what happened, it would sound not that different than the description of a Russian novel.

I'm interested in how you perceive your relation to the world of literary and scholarly journals and magazines that mostly exist for other academics and writers and are essentially unknown to the general public. I know that Grantland *teamed up with* McSweeney's *to release a best-of volume of work. Do you feel like* Grantland *and* McSweeney's *are helping to make the literary world more accessible? Is this a cause that you have any interest in?*

As far as making the literary world more accessible, I would say no because I don't feel that what's on *Grantland* is conventionally literary. It's a literary version of journalism, high-end journalism, but I don't know if it's really up to that standard. *McSweeney's* is a little different. Obviously, if they're putting out Robert Coover books and shit like that, they're involved with literature. But I think for the most part, the kind of people who view themselves as fans of *McSweeney's* are actually more into extensions of the popular culture—the funny little lists they have online, the idea of someone like Dave Eggers, the idea of a literary collective opening a pirate store in Brooklyn.

My relationship to those things is kind of fraught. In the academic world, I think it's troubling to them that my work is so commercially popular. I think what they see it as is a version of academic writing minus the research and the sourcing. There are many, many academics who have written about MTV's *The Real World*. There are no academics whose *Real World* writing would be as known as mine. That's just the way it is. I just sat down and wrote a five-thousand-word essay about *The Real World* and somehow that has more traction than what people have written who studied the semiotics of it. I totally understand why they hate that. It would be no different than if somebody wrote an essay that was just writing the word "puck" over and over again, and then it sold ten times as much as my book. I would think it was crazy.

Sometimes I'll hear that my books are used in college classes. And I really love that. I think it's great. It's really flattering. But am I a creative writer? Or am I a journalist who sometimes does creative writing? Some people think I'm just a music critic and everything else is secondary to that. Some people think I'm mostly a sports writer who also does these other things. I think there's a small percentage of people who think I'm a novelist. So I don't know where I would fit into this world.

Do those classifications matter at all to you? Do you like that you can float in between and do all kinds of different projects?

Totally. I think that anybody would. It's pretty rare that you see someone with a desire to be classified specifically. When I say it's a fraught relationship, that's the downside to the good part of it, which is that I have almost unlimited freedom to do what I want as a creative person.

Do you have a theory why you've become such a popular and well-known writer? Did you ever imagine the level of notoriety you've achieved?

I know I'm supposed to say that I've never thought about it, but of course I have. It's weird to me. It's very odd. It's been, without question, the strangest experience of my life. The fact that in 1999, nobody cared what I thought about anything, not even people in Akron. If I would write a movie review in Akron, nobody took it seriously, nobody was upset by it. Then everything changed. And why did it change? The only thing that really seems to have changed is that people perceive other people as caring. If somebody's reading something I write, it's not that it's necessarily something that to them feels important. It's almost like they make the decision going in—*other people seem to care, so I need to look at this and decide if I agree or disagree.* It's hard for me to know how popular I actually am or am not. It's impossible to know. I can't really tell. It's a confusing thing.

I can see how word of mouth might snowball. But where do you think it started? Is there something you think you do that appeals to a larger audience? Or does it just seem strange and arbitrary to you?

In some ways it's arbitrary. But in another way, I know that it's not. It's arbitrary in the sense that it seems like this could have happened to a lot of different writers, but it just happened to happen to me. Another part of me thinks, *Well, why is that?* I think it could have something to do with the fact that the one thing you can't learn and you can't teach someone is voice. It's just there or isn't. And it seems to be the main thing that people respond to regardless of what that voice is saying. Having a really effective voice as a writer will make people take a bad article more seriously than a well-argued, voiceless article. So I think that my writing is a lot of voice. And I think, with the first two books particularly, I was writing cultural criticism for people who had previously felt totally shut out from that conversation. They would love to read serious, in-depth thoughts about rock music and film and the culture at large. But, for the most part, the people who do that select art that is totally outside of the common experience.

Like, there's so much good writing about the TV show *Girls* right now that it's actually pretty crazy how few people see *Girls*—only people who have HBO, and then a fraction of that audience. I would guess a normal episode of *Girls* is watched by 2.5 million people maybe. That's just a small sliver of people in a huge country. Now all these people are writing these thoughts about *Girls*, and, well, if you haven't seen the show, what are you supposed to do? So what I did is write about the things that were interesting to me, and the reason they were interesting to me is that they were interesting to everybody. That kind of shared culture is so rare now.

This will be my eighth book now. One has been super popular. Every other one has done average to okay. So really it's that one book that's the difference. And maybe it's just because of the title. I don't know.

You've said up to that point essays about pop culture weren't really out there. And now it seems like there is a ton of writing that I think is similar in vein to what you did with Sex, Drugs, and Cocoa Puffs. *Do you feel like you've at all influenced the writing and pop culture world of today? Or do you think it has more to do with the Internet and the fact that more people have a voice and an opportunity to share these kinds of opinions?*

I think timing was a big part of it. I feel like most of what the Internet is writing-wise is criticism of low culture. A lot of it does seem to be written in a very similar style to *Sex, Drugs, and Cocoa Puffs*, which came out in 2002, which is sort of when the Internet took off. I do think that there's probably a relationship there, but I'm hesitant to say that because it could make it seem as if I'm saying, "My book invented the Internet."

You know, I interviewed Richard Linklater one time, and he said something that really stayed with me. I loved *Slacker*. I loved *Dazed and Confused*. I loved all those movies. We were talking about him as a filmmaker, and he said, "Nobody watches my films and thinks, 'That's awesome.' People watch my films and think, 'I can do that.'" I feel like there's a similarity there with *Sex, Drugs, and Cocoa Puffs*. A lot of people love that book because they read it and thought to themselves, *I can do this.*

"A lot of people love *Sex, Drugs, and Cocoa Puffs* because they read it and thought to themselves, *I can do this.*"

When you look back at your career, is there a work of writing that you're most proud of? What would you say has been your most meaningful accomplishment?

Killing Yourself to Live is my favorite of my books. Not because it's the best. But it's kind of the nexus point where I was getting better as a writer, but I was still the same person I was earlier. It's an extremely honest book. I'm not sure I could be that honest now. But I think that from a writerly position, every book seems to have gotten better in terms of how I feel about it. I feel best about the book

I've just done. Next best, about *The Invisible Man*. And so on.

I also really like the very first piece I wrote for *Grantland*. It was about a junior-college basketball game I saw when I was a sophomore in high school. The name of the article is "Three-Man Weave." It's probably the single best thing that I've written. It was a hard story to do. It was hard to find information about this event that happened in the pre-Internet era. It took a long time. I worked on it for a couple of months. I guess I feel good because I felt like I was the only person who could have written this story. I was the only person that would (a) be there, (b) still care about it years later, and (c) be in a position to do the actual writing. That's why I feel good about *Downtown Owl*, too. Not so much because I think it's so brilliant or that it means so much to me personally, but because if I didn't write a book about North Dakota in the '80s, there would never be one. There's nobody else who lived in that time who's a writer now. The whole concept of this pre-cable TV, pre-cell phone, rural, kind of utopia/dystopia, that would not exist. And because I wrote that book, it will always exist. I feel good about that.

What was the genesis for I Wear The Black Hat*?*

It mostly had to do with the fact that as I've aged, I've found something has happened to me, which is that when I was a really little kid, I rooted for heroic figures, then I got a little older and I rooted for anti-heroes and complex heroes, then as I got older still, I started relating to villains in stories. And I wondered why this is and how normal it is. Does this happen to all people as they age or just to me?

Beyond that book, do you have any other projects in the pipeline or any idea of what's next?

I'm still doing *The Ethicist* every week, so that's kind of my main thing now. But in terms of big projects, I'm going to take a little time off. I've published eight books in twelve years. That's not bad. I feel like maybe I went through a phase where I was obsessed with the idea that I was going to lose everything if I stopped, that as soon as I stopped publishing books, the world was going to forget about me and I would go back to whatever my life was like before. Now, I realize that's not really how it works. And also that it's impossible to enjoy your life if you're constantly worried about losing it. I'm just going to try to enjoy my life.

Are there any lifetime-achievement goals that you have? Do you want to write another novel? Is there another type of writing project that you want to take on at some point?

I would just at one point like to write a book that when I go back and read it ten years later, it doesn't seem terrible to me. I've never in my life written something that years later I've felt good about, ever. Maybe I never will. But I think it would be great if I ever did.

Telephone Anger

Summer Pierre

TELEPHONE

ALL DAY LONG THE PAY PHONE BY THE FRONT PARKING LOT RANG. SOMEONE MUST HAVE ANSWERED IT AT SOME POINT. EVERYONE PASSED IT ON THEIR WAY TO CLASS, BUT I NEVER ONCE SAW ANYONE ANSWER IT. I WAS A FRESHMAN, AND NEW TO THE HIGH SCHOOL, SO I DIDN'T YET KNOW ANYONE TO ASK-- BUT WHO CAN RESIST THE LONELY PAY PHONE RINGING FOR LONG? ONE AFTERNOON I STOOD ALONE WAITING FOR MY RIDE WHEN THE PHONE BEGAN TO RING. IT WAS LATE AND NO ONE WAS AROUND -- JUST ME AND THE PHONE. I WALKED OVER TO IT AND WAITED A MOMENT THEN PICKED IT UP. "TOUCH YOURSELF," THE VOICE ON THE OTHER END SAID. IT WAS A QUIET VOICE, A LITTLE UNSURE OF HIMSELF, ALMOST A MUMBLE: "TOUCH YOURSELF," IT SAID WITHOUT NEEDING A HELLO OR GREETING. I SLAMMED DOWN THE PHONE AS IF ELECTROCUTED. 25 YEARS LATER, I CAN STILL REMEMBER THE IMAGE OF A DIM ROOM THAT VOICE CONJURED UP. I SEE THE SHADES DRAWN TO BLOCK OUT THE SUNLIGHT, THE AIR STALE AND THICK. I SHOOK IN MY MINISKIRT AND SNEAKERS BEFORE BOLTING FROM THE SPOT. I RAN TO THE SUNLIT PATCH I HAD BEEN BEFORE AND STOOD WAITING THERE IN THE LIGHT, WHILE THERE IN THE SHADE, THE PHONE SAT AND BEGAN RINGING.

Anger

I KIND OF ENVY PEOPLE WHO GET ANGRY AND HOT, AND PROMPTLY FORGET SOON AFTER -- THEIR CONFLICT OVER AND DONE WITH LIKE A PIECE OF GRIT ALREADY WORKED OVER AND SMOOTHED INTO SOME FORGOTTEN PEARL. I NEVER LEARNED THAT SKILL TO GREET ANGER HEAD ON AND CLEAN. I TRY THIS BUT I FAIL AT IT ALL THE TIME, SOMETIMES LETTING THE RAGE UKNOWINGLY SLIP DOWN INTO MY HEART WHERE IT FESTERS AND BECOMES SOMETHING ELSE: A DEPRESSION, A MEMORY, A SORE MUSCLE, OR A TENDENCY. I FEEL IT NOW START TO REV IT'S ENGINE OVER THE UNFOLDED LAUNDRY, THE CAR WHO TAILS ME, THE EMPTY CARTON OF HALF AND HALF STILL IN THE REFRIGERATOR DOOR -- A MILLION TINY VILLAGES BURST INTO FLAMES INSIDE ME OVER SUCH SIMPLE OCCURRENCES. IT SCARES ME A LITTLE TO THINK WHAT ELSE COULD SET THE FUSE IF I LET IT, BUT WHO AND WHAT BUILT THE BOMB IN THE FIRST PLACE?

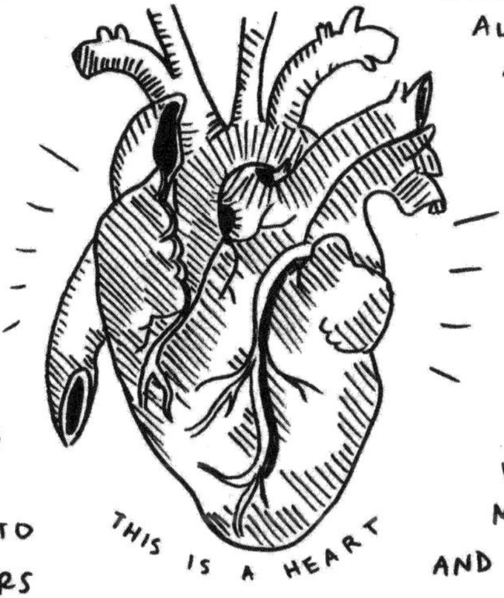

FAMILY
OF
man

Winesburg, Indiana

Michael Martone

Claire Vaye Watkins

Lee Martin

Andrew Hudgins

Porter Shreve

Found in The Placebo: The Yearbook of Emile Durkheim High School

Michael Martone

Carl Frankenstein, Custodian

I am a big man, a big man with an unfortunate name. The embroidery on my uniform stretches way beyond the pocket, over sews the placket. An ugly man who lives alone. A man who will not unlist his home phone number. A man who answers every phone call each night. "Frankenstein," I answer. I hear the murmuring laughs. At halftime of the basketball games, I lumber onto the hardwood with my wide furry mop, up and down the court. The students mob the stands, heave trash into my path. I circle, shaking my fists at the throng in the shadows of the bleachers, the monster that I am. Their monster. After the game, I walk home. I want to mop up the puddles of light cast by the streetlights, sop up the shadows the moon spills in the gutters. At home, I listen to WOWO radio. There are all the scores of all the basketball games in the state that night. I read the phonebook by the fire, chanting those numbers. And before I go to bed, I rip out the stitches of my name from my uniform. Every last thread. I open that old incision over my heart.

Carol App, Truancy Secretary

All day, I make the calls. I check on absences. The rolls come in from the homerooms right after the first bell, collected by dedicated student aides, circulating through the contagious corridors and hallways. The stairwell sings and sewers. Names of the absent. The never-made-it-ins. I contact the contact numbers. I push the number buttons with the eraser on my pencil. No one is home. No one is ever home. Or, no, I imagine them at home in bed, the situation dire. So sick, so stricken that no one can reach the jangling phone on the table next to the sick bed. It rings and rings. Sometime there are ghostly recordings, ghosts in the machine. "We can't make it to the phone right now . . . " I see them wasting away, sweaty in soiled sheets. The stench. The pestilence. Chronic illness is chronic. I put a check mark next to the names, a vector indicating that I will call them back. I call them back. I call them back. Receive the stutter of the persistent ring. Percussive pertussis. A buzz like a biting sting. Allergic to my ear. I am, sad to say, the only one who will receive, in the next hopeful spring, a certificate, one I will make myself, recognizing perfect perfect attendance.

Leslie Sanguine, Cafeteria Cashier

I believe everyone in the school, including the teachers, receives a free or reduced lunch. I am for show, running the old mechanical NCR register, registering the chits and ringing up the dimes. Afterward, I wipe the tables down, restore the order to the condiments, turning the catsup bottles into hourglasses, dripping what's left of one bottle into the leavings of the other. Gravity works, okay? I sweep up the litter of each day's notes that the kids' moms have packed with their cold lunches, little scraps of paper with messages, instructions, prayers. Half-baked home-baked sentiments, fortune cookie scribbles slipped in the pails and sacks. "Try to have a good enough day, Tim!" "Don't fret too much!" "Hope you do a better job in math." "Don't embarrass yourself or us!!!" Or sometimes just a penciled face. One big O with three little o's inside. Oh, oh, oh, oh. My other job—we all work other jobs—is restocking the greeting card concessions in town. The rack at Blister's Pharmacy downtown. Rumi's Cigar Store. Rupp and Otting's Market, the Five and Dime, the news stand in the courthouse run by the blind. I've noticed that the birthday cards, the ones for weddings, new births, anniversaries languish while the get-well ones and the cards of sympathy and bereavement fly out the doors. I work on commission. Pennies a card. After hours, on my hands and knees, I count out from the cartons the somber cards and their dour envelopes and count them into their predetermined slots of the racks. It is like another cafeteria line. Here you go. All the grief you can eat. One more fresh smorgasbord of sad sadnesses.

Howard Junker, Facilities Engineer

My friends call me "How." "How, how you do this?" I get asked all the time. I always know how. How to tape and mud the drywall. How to build a header and shim a door frame. How to wire and plumb. How to snap a plumb line. How to fire the boilers, move the steam. How to make the clocks run on time. My workshop is a shack I built on the roof I roofed. There on my workbench all the guts of the appliances are spread out on the Masonite table I built from scratch. My tools, a silver Milky Way on pegboard. Coffee cans of fasteners. Tupperware tubs of fuses, switches, drawer pulls. I know how to maintain. I know how to maintain. Look! Do you hear that? This mechanical calculator I salvaged from Mr. Rice's physics lab thirty years ago is still running. Big as a breadbox, studded and stuttering with gears and ratchets and armatures and levers, it has been sawing away all that time. Long ago, I told the machine to perform an impossible task. I divided a whole number by 0 and the contraption's workings have been searching all this time (in the toothed flanges, greased widgets, stripped screws) for the mechanical expression of infinity. The machine makes a racket as it calibrates, clucking and clunking, at any moment on the edge of entropy, unengineering itself, a twitching pile of junk. But it goes on and on. How does it do it? I maintain it. I tend to it. It will keep looking for infinity forever. Forever forever. It is a little engine that asks how how how how. How's time machine telling time.

Mari, Waiting

Claire Vaye Watkins

A wife waits for her husband, a wife waits for her husband.

Mari whose name is not Mari waits for Gus whose name is not Gus.

(Mary waits for Gursnan.)

Mari waits for Gus, her husband, though she's not yet used to the word.

A *wife* waits at the window for her *husband*, though they have not uttered these terms since the interview.

A wife in contract but not in covenant, a wife in status, a wife in stasis, a wife in ink and pixel—not loin, not bone—a wife like scissors for red tape, a wife beneath a loophole arbor dripping with marsh marigolds and lady's slipper and pasture roses worn wide by a pageant of loveless lovers walking arm-in-arm, waits.

Mari waits for Gus at the window, practicing—*This is Gus, my* husband. *My* husband *has not eaten for twenty days. My* husband *does not plan to eat for fifteen more.*

A wife waits for her husband to come home from a run.

Mari waits at the sink while Gus—twiggy brown hull—jogs in slow motion, jogs as an old man wind-up toy might jog, jogs as Go-Go Gandhi might if Gandhi had a new pair of Brooks Adrenaline GTS 12s, jogs into Winesburg and out the other side, though his *wife* has asked him not to jog there.

Mari waits and waiting with her is Gus, the ghost of him, the cartoon silhouette: short, silky, and regal purple running shorts, and beneath those his special cotton underwear that poke out the bottom a little and have a drawstring, his bare boy's chest, his tiny lavender nipples, his pinched taut abdomen, his hard outie, his black mist of beard, his lovely and bulbous marigold turban with its secret wooden comb tucked inside, his brown legs pistons, his brown arms thew, his go belt strapped around his hips, hung with plastic globules filled with water and his crescent dagger in its sheath, his polished silver kara around his wrist, tinking lightly against his stopwatch.

Though she has asked him not to, Gus jogs frail past the county park and the Catholic school and the Winesburg Diner and the Dollar General and the closed Circuit City where they were best friends before they were play pretend spouses and Karl's Finer Food and Martin's Grocery and the house where Mari grew up with her mother inside making ham salad and sighing over the curious decisions of an undutiful daughter and the slaughterhouse and the Target glowing in the dusk like all those spaceships landed in all those cornfields, while Mari waits.

Mari waits at the end of the driveway with a fresh, sweating water bottle, a few drops of lemon juice added in secret.

In secret, Mari waits for Gus, waits to pluck the cicadas from his sweat-glistening back, waits to scoop the gnats from his eyes.

Mari waits and waits and waits while duallies downshift and open up the sky and thunder too near Gus, waits while boys she went to high school with shout, *raghead* and *faggot* and *sand nigger.*

Mari—kneeling at the tub, rinsing in hot water yards and yards of supple saffron fabric that sway like water plants, losing and finding her hands in them, scraping with her square, unpainted fingernails crusted pink flagella where a gallon of strawberry ice cream launched from a Cummins Diesel detonated in front of Gus, recalling how he came home early with fat carpenter bees wafting behind him, recalling how she had wanted very badly to lick him clean—waits.

Mari at the window, Mari at the drive, Mari at the bathtub, and Mari in the bedroom, stringing damp fabric to dry around the room where the night before Gus stood in his special cotton underwear—a gift from God. But wasn't everything?—telling how the knot at the drawstring was there to thwart lustful thoughts, to remind the faithful to think of members of the opposite sex as they would a family member, *Like you, Mari, you're like a sister to me,* then Gus unknotting the knot and saying how to test himself, Gandhi used to sleep nude with his grandniece, and holding Mari from behind, Gus sliding his smooth penis up and down between her fat-dappled butt cheeks, waiting.

Mari waits for Gus to leave her, Mari waits for Gus to love her.

Mari waits for Gus to stand up too quickly, waits for him to faint, because when he falls he falls silent as a pile of laundry and she sits on the floor and puts his swaddled head in her lap and kisses him.

Mari waits, though for what she does not know.

Miss Gladys

Lee Martin

Mornings, this autumn, I see the girls skipping past on their way to school, and my heart lifts at the sound of their bright voices. I live at the end of Locust Street in a one-story frame house with a porch that wraps around the side. If visitors know me, they knock on the side door when they come, aware that I spend most of my time in the dining room where I have my television set and the oak drop-leaf table I inherited from my mother, and the rocking chair, reupholstered now, that belonged to my father. I sit at the table working a crossword. The television is on for the noise, usually some sort of news show on CNN because I like to keep up to date. I may be on the far side of eighty, but I'm not dead yet. The world can still amaze me.

This morning, I hear a voice outside my window—a light, thin voice singing that old kids' song, "Itsy Bitsy Spider." I glance up from my puzzle, and I see the girl, no more than nine or ten, coming up the steps toward my front door. It's one of those cloudless September days when the air is so clear, the slightest sound carries. Crows caw from the oak trees where the leaves are just now tinged with red. A car door slams somewhere up the street. The last bell rings at Winesburg Elementary, where once upon a time I taught, and I hear it plain as day.

"You're late for school," I say to the girl when I open the front door.

"I'm on my way," she says, not flustered a bit, and for a moment I remember the girl I was, head in the stars, chin leading forward, ready to make my life.

"You want to buy this?" She holds on her palm a figurine made from spun glass, a pale blue hummingbird, wings open, its beak probing a petunia bloom. The beak is short and too flat. The bird's eyes are too far apart, and, well, truth be told, the whole thing is a mess. The head is too big, the body too arched in an attempt to make it seem that the bird is hovering over the petunia. The bird actually seems to be smiling, and I can't decide whether it looks more like a dolphin or maybe a cross between a dolphin and a platypus.

"My daddy made it," the girl says.

"Does your daddy need glasses?" I can't help myself. It's said before I can stop it. "You ought to get to school."

The girl tips back her head a tad, squints at me, then says in a very measured voice, "You ought not to be such a mean old bitch."

Maybe I fall in love with her a little, as much charmed as I am shocked by how she comes back at me like that. What can I do but buy the figurine—five dollars, she wants for it.

"What are you going to do with that money?" I ask her.

She folds the bill and sticks it into her jacket pocket. It's a thin denim jacket, short in the waist, and faded from too many washings. Frayed threads, nearly white, unravel from the collar and the cuffs. She stuffs her fists into her pockets and shrugs her shoulders—such a slight, delicate girl with a long neck and fine blonde hair, blue veins showing through the white skin of her eyelids.

"Guess I'll know that when I've got enough," she says.

She smells like old cooking oil and black bananas and wet dirt. I can't place her from any of the houses nearby; could be she lives in one of the trailers the next street over. A smudge of something dark shadows the left corner of her mouth. When she catches me looking at that stain with a disapproving frown, she tucks her head down and rubs her jaw across her shoulder.

"How will you know when you have enough?"

She shrugs again. "Just will. You want me to come back tomorrow?" She smiles at me so sweetly. "I'll bring you another pretty."

"And want another five dollars, I suppose?"

She doesn't flinch. "Pretty is as pretty costs."

"You think five dollars makes that hummingbird look any less like a platypus?"

I don't let her know that she's shaken me. My breath is catching in my throat. I feel like my legs might give way. I've only heard someone change up that old saw about pretty is as pretty does one other time in my life, but now this girl has said it—pretty is as pretty *costs*—and just like that I'm back over sixty years ago in the cafe by the Winesburg train station—The White Spot—and I've just ordered a piece of coconut cream pie.

It was August, the dog days, and I was having lunch before going back to my summer job at the Rexall drug store. I worked the cash register and stocked shelves when business was slow. Sometimes I delivered medicines to customers who were housebound, folks as old as I am now. The pharmacist, Mr. Lister, called me his girl. "I'll send my girl right over with your heart pills," he'd tell someone on the phone. "What's that? Oh, yes, she's a good girl. Very dependable. She'll be there in a jiff."

That day at The White Spot, I was bored, and only a week away from the end of that summer job. I was eager to be back at Oakland City College, where I was studying to be an elementary school teacher. All summer, as customers had come and gone, I'd felt Winesburg close around me. My job gave me too much intimacy with people and their infirmities and habits. I knew who suffered from gout, lumbago, insomnia, heart palpitations, dyspepsia, toe-nail fungus, athlete's foot, ringworm, vertigo. I knew the women who colored their hair, the teenagers who smoked Chesterfields and Pall Malls, the men who wore trusses and sometimes took penicillin for matters better left undisclosed. I knew all this, and it was too much to know. It left me longing for someone who could be a mystery to me, someone I could know a little bit at a time and never feel like I knew everything.

Then I ordered that piece of coconut cream pie, and the waitress, Meryl Lane, who came into the Rexall each month to buy the new *True Confessions* magazine—she'd been reading the August issue when I'd sat down at the lunch counter; I'd seen it open to an article titled, "I Couldn't Forgive My Brother-in-Law"—told me that the man at the other end of the lunch counter had just ordered the last piece of pie. A man in a light blue seersucker suit and a red and navy bowtie. A stranger with a yellow-cream leather suitcase on the floor by his stool. A pretty man with black hair, oiled and combed. He looked at me and smiled, and I felt my heart go.

"Why don't we split it?" he said. "Go halvsies. You game?"

I was indeed. I picked up my hatbox pocketbook, let it swing in my hand by its Lucite handle, and I strolled down the line of counter stools. My dress was new, a lavender summer dress with white polka dots, and a circle skirt with a ruffled hem. I liked the way the ruched bust flattered me, and I hoped this man would like it, too. I took my time as if I knew exactly where I was going and didn't need to hurry.

Turned out, I didn't know a thing.

A piece of coconut cream pie. A man with time to kill while he waited on his train, a girl with her head in the clouds and eager for her real life to begin.

I stand here now toward the end of that life, and I can remember the way the air felt when the man and I stepped outside The White Spot—heavy with humidity, the sky overcast, and everything so still the way it is when a storm is coming. Locusts chirred. The couplings of boxcars clanked together in the rail yards behind the station. A smell of old flowers and dried cornstalks and river water told me autumn was coming soon.

What did we do? That man and I? I took his hand. I led him down the alley and up the stairs to the room above the Rexall that Mr. Lister used for storage. I shut the door behind us, and I didn't turn on the light.

The man set down his yellow-cream suitcase.

"Do you like my dress?" I said. "Do you think it's pretty?"

He moved in close to me. He put his hands on my waist. "Pretty is as pretty costs," he said.

He moved his hand up under my skirt, and I let him. I didn't know everything that would follow. I didn't know that my life had already started to change. I didn't know that come spring, I'd be at the Nebraska Children's Home in Omaha, saying goodbye to my newborn daughter. I didn't know I'd never marry, didn't know I'd spend my life taking care of other women's children. To me, it was just a late-summer afternoon in Winesburg. I was just an antsy girl, too daring for her own good, too brazen. I had my whole life ahead of me.

Now, the girl in my house looks up at me, her chin quivering and turning to gooseflesh. "It's a hummingbird," she says. "A goddamn hummingbird. Are you blind? Anyone can see that."

I tell her to come back tomorrow, and to bring me another pretty. "I'll pay." She turns and runs out of my house, down my steps, up the sidewalk to school. All I can do is step out onto my porch and call after her. "You just tell me how much." I watch until I can't see her anymore. "I'll pay whatever it costs."

But she's gone, so I go back into my dining room, where I set the hummingbird figurine on top of my television.

CNN tells me that the United Nations will try to resolve the Syrian government's bloody offensive against its citizens; unease continues in Egypt; the rapper 50 Cent is visiting impoverished sites in Kenya and Somalia; the Human Rights Watch calls for Iraqi officials to stop executing prisoners; the Mexican army has seized more than fifteen tons of methamphetamine from a clandestine laboratory in a remote area of the state of Jalisco.

Meanwhile, I'm living through another day in Winesburg, already thinking about bedtime when I'll lie down to sleep. I like to let the world get by on its own for a few hours, but sometimes I think about the man with the yellow-cream suitcase and the daughter he never knew existed. I hope she has a happy life. I hope the thought of me doesn't bear upon her. I say a little prayer for her, and one for the girl with the hummingbird figurine. Then I let it all go—the things I can't change—and all morning I watch the way the sunlight splinters through the spun glass of that figurine, sending spots of color wheeling across my floor, my wall. I almost believe I can reach out and hold them in my hand.

Raymond Snow

Andrew Hudgins

I was wearing mittens because the warehouse was cold as hell so maybe I didn't have as good a grip on the forklift's wheel as I thought I did when I slipped my blades into the skip, and somebody must have got the load off-center because when I lifted, the forks hadn't gone all the way in, and the TVs—the flat screens, plasmas break if you just fart in their general direction—sort of slouched on the pallet at about three feet up. So I sped up to try to force the fork all the way in. That's when I kinda tossed 'em into the shelving unit that tipped and hit another shelving unit that tipped too, but luckily there was a wall next, so it wasn't nearly as bad as it could have been.

Well, that's what they have insurance for.

Foreman, that was Wally, kept screaming words like stupid and drunk and shit like that but he got quiet when Mr. Hansen pulled up to the overhead door in that big turd-brown 1980s Cadillac because he—I mean Wally—was starting to remember that there were two joints smoked out in his car before the shift started and I'd only smoked one though I'd paid for two, though he did let me have a couple of chugs from the bottle of Beam he keeps under the front seat so it sort of evens out maybe. Once they got to asking questions they might want to know if any of that Schedule 20 stainless pipe that was short on the last inventory and that Mr. Hansen wouldn't stop bitching about was maybe under a tarp back of somebody's garage and I don't have a garage.

I was fired and all that shit, who's surprised? But I came back a couple of weeks later to eat lunch with the guys cause I thought Wally might help me find another job for keeping my mouth shut and all, but I saw that wasn't never going to happen. Before we even got to the break room, I was standing next to him at the urinal, and he nodded up at the ceiling with his chin and said, It must suck to be the asshole who has to sit all day and watch us pee.

I said, Wha'?

And he said, Since you left they been watching us all the time. Wired the whole damn place, putting in cameras. Didn't make no secret of it.

But they can't do it in here, can they?

Not *legally.*

So for help I went to Brenda, the blond girl I was chasing then and not getting much of nowhere—hair so white it looked fake because it was fake, but hell she was trying. She helped me get on doing night clean up at Hendry's IGA and that wasn't so bad because it's small and the butchers do all their own clean up. That's the worst stuff mostly, 'cept for the toilets, and ain't but two of those and they aren't for customers, so you know who's using them and they know you know, and I don't mind calling them out about piss on the floor if I have to. So I ate pretty good for a couple of months going toward spring—mostly just sliced bread and lunch meat, nothing too big—when I started seeing this little brunette. Bit of a mistake that one, freckly girl, single again at forty and ready for it though she moaned a lot about when I was going to sleep over at her house like I was all excited about walking out of her bedroom in the morning and grinning an I-been-boning-your-mom grin at a seventeen-year-old boy forty pounds bigger than me and lettering in football and felonious assault. Brenda didn't get me fired about the brunette, but she did put the night manager on alert so I had to start buying my own food, which was like taking a pay cut.

But here's the whole point I've been getting to, which was that I brought Brenda, once we got back together for awhile, to Fourth of July at my rich cousin Robert's place out in the country because it was his turn and he owns his house. Been Bobby till he got to high school, then he was Bob. But go to law school and make a fortune putting criminals back on the street and you become Robert and don't have to listen when somebody calls you Bobby even though he drug you out of your granddaddy's oak tree when your ladder fell over and you'd been up there crying for three hours like a baby. Even fetched down his damn wind-up plastic airplane for his little crybaby ass.

They set us at the porch table with the children and Stevey, and his wife whose name I never can remember, something like Will Fred. That's not it exactly, but it's what I call her. She answers to it. And just as soon as I took a big bite of rich-cousin hamburger and started chewing, Stevey says in that slow retarded way of his, I wan you stop tell people I retarded.

I never told no one you a retard, Stevey, I said, and Brenda looked at me funny, which reminded me I had told her and done a little imitation too, which she didn't like but her brothers laughed at it pretty good.

Let's be clear here. Stevey *is* a retard. He worked in the sheltered workshop for a year—it's where he met his wife—before they got him that job at

Circle K he's had for like ten years. Daddy always said Stevey had a certificate from the state proving he was a retard but I've never seen it. It's not exactly something you bring out when rich cousin Robert is showing everybody *Winesburg Argus* clippings about every base hit his boy made or the ribbons his girls won in horse jumping.

Mr. smuh, smuh, shuh—Mr. Smitherman at work tole me you tole ev'body at your work I wah retard.

Then Mr. Smuh's a liar.

He said I han't drop pah, pah, pallet TVs.

The retard wife and the kids at the table started giggling till I stood up, and just as I was trying to decide if I should hit him or kick the table over, Robert put his hand on my shoulder and said, Why don't you do what Steve asks and not talk about him. That'd be like a kindness to everyone, don't you think? Let's go see if there's another one of those—whatcha got there, Molsons? So I picked up the rest of my burger and followed him to get a beer I didn't have much taste for anymore because he was right that you shouldn't torment the less fortunate. I did motion Brenda in front of me, gentleman like, before I turned back and kinda swept my eyes over Stevey and Will Fred and them kids too so they'd know Uncle Ray hadn't forgot nothing. Over by the beer tub, I could tell Robert wanted to say something more, so I just took a couple of Molsons in each hand and led Brenda straight to the truck. Told Brenda she should take a couple too but she said, No, I don't think so.

"Manchild" Morrison, the Best That Almost Was

Porter Shreve

Every ten years they trot me out for homecoming. Put me in the back of a red convertible and drive me around the stadium where half a century ago I took the Railsplitters to our first and only state championship. We ran the single wing back then, the old "Pop" Warner formation, with four guys in the backfield, any one of us ready for the snap. But in 1962, in Winesburg, Indiana, everyone knew the ball was going to number 21. I might as well have had a target on my jersey.

I don't remember how I got the nickname, "Manchild." It used to drive my mother crazy.

He's Donald, for the love of Pete.

What are you feeding him, Mrs. Morrison?

Her Irish cheeks would glow as red as twisted apples.

I was always big for my age. A twelve-pound baby, a head taller than my classmates in all the pictures. In seventh grade I played varsity basketball. In eighth the football coach suited me up, and the rest is history. To this day I hold every school record: rushing touchdowns, touchdown passes, all-purpose yards. I have all the kicking records, too. Once, before practice, I knocked a fifty-eight yarder through the goal posts, but it wasn't such a feat: the wind was at my back and the ball nicked the crossbar on its way through.

He's just being modest, people would say when I'd tell them I wasn't that good, but it turned out I was right. Never made the pros. Ask anyone outside the county if they've heard of "Manchild" Morrison and you'll get a nod from a Purdue diehard or two who remembered the hype that followed my signing. "The Best That Almost Was," ran the headline in the *Indianapolis Star* the week after I blew out my knee in a scrimmage freshman year.

People tell me I would have played alongside Bob Griese, another in-state hotshot who would go on to All American, then quarterback for the Miami Dolphins, winner of two Super Bowls and owner to this day of the last undefeated season in pro football.

Undefeated. Imagine.

I never did finish at Purdue. Got the surgery, but doctors were stabbing in the dark in 1963. They stapled the ends of the ligament together and one afternoon, on a rehab jog around the track, I felt a ping, then collapsed on the asphalt. I was no Gale Sayers. I wasn't coming even halfway back from that. So I dropped out and headed home to Winesburg, sat around for a year or two feeling sorry for myself, gained forty pounds on sympathy casseroles. I hung a map of the U.S. on my bedroom wall, put pins in the states I'd visited—the Great Lakes eight, plus four in the South from a family trip to New Orleans. Twelve down, thirty-eight to go. Then the center on the old team, Tommy Flynn, who had just finished up at DePauw, proposed we go into business together. All I had to do was lend my name and look the part of local legend, and we'd have it made.

"Manchild" Motors: New and Used. Tommy was right, for a time. We did a good business. I worked the door, he did the selling, and his sunny wife, Cheryl, kept the books. They had twin boys and bought a five-bedroom house on a man-made lake in Whispering Woods. But one day, out for a test drive (he loved to see which was the fastest car on the lot), Tommy flipped a Camaro on the river road and went off to join James Dean. I was left with a car dealership, a grieving widow, and little idea of what to do with either. Six months after the funeral, Cheryl and I were going over inventory in her office when she put her hand on my cheek. I still remember the photo on her desk of Tommy and the kids peering at us, as if through a window. We married, divorced, remarried, and now we're separated again. I haven't spoken with her since spring.

Which brings me more or less to this morning, when I found myself standing at the bathroom mirror of the Extended Stay in my fifty-year-old high school uniform, the 21 as yellow as my teeth against the faded crimson. Coach Keller Jr. had asked me to wear the old jersey again. He'd done the same for the fortieth anniversary homecoming, as had his dad, Coach Keller Sr., for the thirtieth, twentieth, and tenth. I'll admit that I've tried on the uniform over the years, and not just before these games. But it never fit, so in the past I went in a windbreaker with the dealership's logo on the back—a red Mustang flying through goalposts.

This time, though, the jersey slid right on. In fact, it drooped over my shoulders and arms; I looked like an old man playing dress-up. If I'd opened the door to such a sight on Halloween, I'd have felt a shiver. The whole town would be there. Cheryl. The twins, their wives and kids. No one missed a homecoming, and this was the golden anniversary of the once and forever golden age. I've seen more people in the dealership over the last few months than I have in years. But they haven't been buying cars. They go online or drive to volume lots in Indy or Fort Wayne. I used to move fifty cars a month. Now I'd be lucky to sell five. I should have changed the name years ago. People who actually watched "Manchild" Morrison smash through a defensive line and drag cornerbacks downfield like strings of cans are dying every week. Parents. Uncles and aunts. Teachers. Shopkeepers. Classmates. I used to go to their memorials but lately I'd rather not be seen.

It was Cheryl who first mentioned the weight loss. She made me stand on her bathroom scale. Two hundred forty, down twenty pounds from normal. I hadn't been to the doctor in five years, and my refusal after the scale's needle kept marching west—now under two hundred for the first time since I was a kid—opened up old hurts in Cheryl that made her impossible to live with. Anything would set her off. A coffee mug I hadn't rinsed out. Empty trash cans too long at the curb. The way I'd forget to switch stations when commercials came on. *Earth to Donald*, she said. And when I still wouldn't go to the doctor after months of Cheryl's nagging, she gave me one last chance. Called in the appointment herself, wrote it down in big letters on the kitchen calendar. *11:30 a.m. Dr. Reeves. You go, or I go*, she said. *I'm not going to be a widow two times over.*

I went to work, and I swear I had every intention of driving over to the internist's. But I had a customer who was hot to buy a new Chrysler 300, and we were negotiating, me holding firm, stepping away to the back office to stall the guy. It was noon when we closed the deal, my first and last of that week. Cheryl asked me to move out the next day.

I haven't stepped on a scale since, but I can feel myself shrinking. I drove forty-five miles to the outlet mall to buy clothes that would fit, and the expressions of people who come in to the dealership tell me all I need to know.

They're too polite to ask, *What happened to the rest of you?* Or to say, *You're getting treatment, I assume?* I don't trust doctors, but that's not the real issue. If I made another appointment, if I stood up in the waiting room when the nurse called, *Mr. Morrison*, and went through that door to the steel table, I'd be interrupting the natural course of events. I remember Cheryl once asking, *Do you ever wonder what would have happened if you hadn't played in that scrimmage, or if the ball had gone to someone else on that particular down? You might not have come home. We might never have met. Tommy and I might have been watching you on TV, inviting people over on Sundays to brag on you and talk about the '62 team.*

I don't think about that stuff, I said. *What's meant to be is meant to be.*

I remember another time, after I'd dropped out of college, my mother coming into my room one afternoon when I'd been sleeping most of the day:

What are you going to do? she asked.

I guess we'll see what happens, I said.

You sound just like your father.

How would I know?

My father drove a '51 Windsor convertible. My mother used to call it his mistress. The lady in red. I was too young to understand what she meant, but I can picture him now, out on the driveway polishing the hood, bent close enough to see his reflection. Just as my mother might have predicted, he did run off with that car. He used to talk about California, but he only got as far as Casper, Wyoming, before he ran out of money or nerve. He did roustabout work in the oil fields, made journeyman then foreman at the Amoco refinery, died of a heart attack on the job nine months short of retirement.

I don't know if Coach Keller has heard the details of that story—surely so, in a town like this—but of all the cars on the lot he always asks me to bring a red convertible for my little halftime parade around the track. And I say sure. But this year I must have forgotten to order a red convertible because the only soft top we have in stock is black, with tinted windows. I grab the keys, toss the old jersey in the passenger seat, and fire up the engine. Though it's a perfect fall evening, I keep the top up for now. It's eight o'clock. Homecoming Friday. The streets are dim and empty. Closed signs glow in the restaurant windows. I could run the red lights, strip naked and race down Main Street crying *Hallelujah*, and no one would see or care because they're all at the football stadium.

By the time I drive up near the entrance, it's late in the second quarter and the place is packed to the gills. I cut the motor, crack the window to let in the cool breeze, the smell of popcorn, cotton candy, raked leaves, and hormones. The crack of helmets and pads, waves of cheers, whistles, air horn blasts sweep in. The school band, forever out of tune, plays "We Will Rock You," and cheerleaders shoot into the air like fireworks. Coach Keller paces the sidelines, tugging at his headset. And I can see gathered behind him, lined up in the stands, some of the old-timers—my teammates—wearing their faded jerseys. A few of them are shifting around, seeming anxious, as if on the lookout for someone.

The universal rule of homecoming games is that you schedule a team you can beat, but the Railsplitters are down 24-3. I'm checking the clock on the scoreboard and getting ready to pop the top of the convertible—I've already got my fingers on the release handle—when I see one of the old-timers point in my direction. He must have ESP, because I'm a good fifty yards away in a hearse-black car with tinted windows double parked outside the chain-link fence. Then someone else is looking over and others are pointing, too, and it's like I'm watching a Western in slow motion about a posse of retired lawmen who have come together for one last ride. They've stepped off the bleachers and are walking toward me, coming around the track, past the end zone and the concession stand. I let go of the release handle and turn the ignition. Before I roll up the window, I reach into the passenger seat and grab my old jersey. I toss the thing out onto the sidewalk, where it lands flat on its back, arms stretched out, as if steamrolled by tacklers.

I throw the car in drive and floor it. I peel out of there like a joyriding teenager. Squealing tires. Fishtailing. Leaving marks on the street. I don't slow down for lights or anything. I fly through town out onto the river road, and up the ramp to the interstate, headlights stiff arming the darkness. Nothing in front of me but open lanes, an empty map. I step on the gas, like Tommy Flynn, like the "Manchild" Morrison of old: football star. Can't stop me now. I'm going, going. Good as gone.

Fire Season

Suzanne Richardson

In moth season I levitate because of a married man,
the sound of my own desire keeps
me awake at night, keeps me tossing four feet
above the sheets, I imagine us powder-thrashing
like moths at a screen—

On the roof of his car, off route 14,
it feels like 1955. We watch the moon squeeze itself
between the earth and the sun. It's
hallucinatory, the sun is a shrinking slice of light. We
can't touch. I am already casting hell-grey shadows,
eclipsing his wife. It's so devastating
we must not look directly.
His voice, *If I live my life right, I'll die on the moon*
looking at the earth,
looking at all the people I love, and all the people
I once loved. A married man
pushes the atmosphere and I levitate above
the forest, this moth season behind me,
he murmurs—*soon this will all be on fire.*

Learn The Dark

Suzanne Richardson

I haunt
the streets where I wonder if
my former lovers feel my
planetary pull. I am trapped between
two moons: you tell me if I were a man
and you were a woman you'd
let me touch your body tonight. I feel
my own fish squirming, and
your hands, batwings, pulse and
peel open—
we don't touch.
I go to the graveyard searching for meaning.
I go to hear all the death: little Eliza Olin, gone
since 1832, and me so alive; I must spook her.
Then—
—body noise: breath   moving   liquid.
And I hear all the life:
the orgasms blinking outward
like rescue signals at dawn. Men fucking
by the precious headstones of the orphans.
a slip, a grind, a burn, okay—
Only when I am this thirsty do I

drink the spit of strangers. Later, I
dreamt your wet stretches
of saliva fell into me; you
let the bulbs burn out, opened
your mouth, and let me learn the dark.

Rabbit Season

Suzanne Richardson

Years before we met, we
imagined the same rabbit
thumping a salt bush—conejo you
whispered deep into
your desk drawer, the sound split
my head, like how
a rock diverts rivers. I
am your thorny
little sister not your lover. I
watched you jump
at every skirt but mine. Later, I
throw up green in your juniper bush
while your lover tells me I
am so good, so quiet when I
reveal what's inside. Brother,
last I heard, you watched a rabbit die
its head bashed purple on a fence post,
it was something I couldn't imagine.

V

Sarah Heffner

The shape of migrating birds at her mouth
She tells me   North America is south

For some birds   She is named after
The tips of leaves

All this time I had been rubbing
Boats together   stern to stern

I woke up to bird watching
My mouth all over the bed

A Borrowed Childhood Memory, Alloway, 4 July 1967

Mark Jay Brewin Jr.

for my father

Fire and strike sevenfold. Salute and witness the grown-ups
whiskey stagger around the farmstead and backfield.
Crawl among the knee-grass, throw rotting beefsteak
tomatoes at your cousins. When hit, yell, *I'm going down . . .*

Skitter along the cow fence, into your uncle's barn,
watch him lop off horns with crank shears, the fresh
blunted skull crowns, the glossy spurt, blood
beading down the heifers' flanks. When asked, stop

your ears with newspaper pages, climb barn rafters.
Play back what they said, how they said it, *Do it, boy. Go on,*
and spook the pigeons without falling, while they
pick them off, one by one, with a .22—don't slip, breathe

through your mouth so you don't smell the cat piss.
Wait, alone, for hours—fireworks aren't something to miss.

State Forests

David Ryan

I saw him standing on the Ward's Island Bridge and had to resist the urge to just stop and watch. I thought he might jump. So I climbed the ladder to the crosswalk and started walking toward him. It felt impulsive and slow at the same time—maybe it was just the heat that day, like there was a suddenness, but it was on a seven-second delay. I was sweating by the time I came near. I shouted something, some sort of nonsense; it could have been anything.

The air felt thinner above the river. The water below roared in ways you never hear from the ground. The sound of traffic carried with the water, as if the traffic and the river were both shouting up, as if when you listened and tried to untwine all the strands of sound you could hear *Jump* coming from below. Or maybe I said, *Jump*, even as I meant to say, *Don't jump*. Maybe *Don't* had gotten tangled up in the city sounds. I don't know. I had wanted to discourage him, to say something about being alive still. At least in the beginning. But then he was laughing. The man was laughing. *Jump? Jump?* he said. He'd heard the river too. Or was he laughing at me?

—I thought you were going to jump, I said. I was close enough to grab him, if I had wanted.

—I'm just taking in the view. His voice sounded exactly like mine, it had the same timbre, the same inflection. The water below seemed fraught with itself, breathless.

—It's quite a view, I admitted.

Did he say anything? We were watching a helicopter above Williamsburg now. It wasn't any bigger than a fly. It approached, dangling over the water—steady, bigger now, like a dragonfly, then rearing overhead like a dragon, then away and off like a dragonfly again, then, north. Over Queens it was just a fly again, and then it was just a fleck of ash.

Traffic had stopped. People were getting out of their cars and shouting, *Don't jump*, or something. The way the sound rose, you could just hear *Jump*—you could feel all the desire gathering up with the roar of the river, chaotic and musical.

—I drove a taxi all through grad school, he said. I always hated that parkway.

—Sometimes I drive around all day, I said: I'll just take a rental out upstate, drive around like I'm still married, like we're looking for a place to spend a few hours.

—Those were the days.

—A nice forest preserve, someplace like that, I said.

We jumped. Or, at least, we were no longer standing on the bridge. The fall seemed to never end. We were in a free fall. It felt perpetual, binding. The wind roared, like it had jumped along with us.

—We were married there, you know. My wife and I.

—There? he asked.

I pointed:

—Carl Schurz Park—over the underpass where all the traffic has stopped. It was a lovely wedding, I said.

—I don't doubt it, he said. It's where the mayor lives, after all.

—I wonder will the water be cold, I said. I suppose I was just trying to keep conversation up. Trying to keep our minds occupied.

—I never married, he said. I think I would have had an Episcopalian service. Big church. Doleful bells. He seemed lost in thought.

For how long we fell I don't know. I put on weight and my hair thinned and grayed. We lost interest in each other's conversation. We flew into little silent rages and moments of extraordinary gratefulness. It was hard to talk over the roar of the approaching water but, you know, you get used to shouting. You forget the water. You just keep falling and falling. I woke a thousand times. I dreamed about driving for miles and miles, looking for state forests, places to stop. Places with names: Loyalsock, Susquehannock, Hogsback. Would the river smash us like stone? Would our hearts explode instead, before we hit the surface?

> "For how long we fell I don't know. I put on weight and my hair thinned and grayed."

He was singing *Wild geese that fly with the moon on their wings . . .*

—Never had kids, I shouted. I saw my wife somewhere waiting up. I saw her writing down names. Now the harder edges of the city had turned to dust, its yellow ghosts hung shapeless in the ozone. The skyline looked like a diorama some neighbor kid had smashed up. Like you come home from work and there's this strange kid sitting in your living room, and there's a skyline all over the floor.

I thought about an old joke I still found funny. Joke still made me laugh. Then I realized that I had misunderstood what had been funny about it. It had taken all these years. All along the thing had just flown over my head. And still, even now, I found myself laughing.

I had an unrelated thought. I closed my eyes and it was gone.

How I Write

Chris Offutt

Kim Addonizio

Pam Houston

Josh Neufeld

Katharine Rauk

Matt Bell

CHRIS OFFUTT

I've used the same desk setup for over twenty years—a four-by-eight sheet of plywood, three-quarters of an inch thick, finished on one side, placed over two filing cabinets twenty-five inches high. I cut a rectangular gap in the long side, twenty-one inches by thirty-two inches, and finished the rough edges with trim. I sit in the notch. The precise measurements came from my sitting height, arm's length, and relationship of legs to floor. I sit in an ergonomic chair and use an ergonomic keyboard. Unfortunately I slouch terribly, which pretty much destroys all the effort.

CHRIS OFFUTT'S DESK, 2013.

"My goal is to write one minute per day and I always achieve that goal."

I always place my desk in a corner and use the walls as a bulletin board. I prefer a window to my left. I use two copy stands for transcribing. My desk is laden with lucky talismans I've found in the woods—mostly rock, feather, and wood. A bag of dirt from Kentucky. A few animal skulls. A dictionary and thesaurus are at hand, along with thirty reference books about nature. My goal is to write one minute per day and I always achieve that goal. After about three hours of writing new material, I stop.

I can revise for much longer. I never revise before finishing a draft. My revisions are heavy, with many drafts. As I've gotten older, I write fewer drafts, but the early ones are stronger. Experience has paid off. My typing is better, too.

I always write first thing in the morning. My mind is freshest after a night's rest. If I write first, before any other task, I feel good about myself for the rest of the day. If I put off writing, the risk is never getting to it.

CHRIS OFFUTT'S DESK, 1985.

I carry pen and paper everywhere always. If I hear, see, or think of something interesting, I write it down. Later I move those scraps to a notebook and use them in my work. My journals go back forty-five years. They're boring and poorly written. I seem to have matured very little and still complain about the same things I did at age ten.

I read two or three books a week. I try to avoid television and movies, social media, and videogames. I don't drink hard alcohol, smoke marijuana, or use drugs. I have quit cigarettes about twenty times. My main tools are time and my mind, and I try not to squander either one too much.

I've always feared repeating myself. To avoid that, I write in different forms—essay, story, novel, screenplay, comic book, memoir. Each new project requires a new approach. I rearrange my writing studio before each one. For novels I outline. For screenplays I outline heavily. With essays and short fiction, I start with a vague idea or image and jump right in.

Most importantly of all, I live very cheap and have never taken a full-time job. I buy everything used. I never went into credit-card debt.

Every day I just sit down and try hard.

KIM ADDONIZIO

I write by osmosis. I write by divine decree. I write by heart, the heart shaking itself off like a dog that has nearly drowned in light. Or the heart dimly lit, sputtering and darkening, the heart shattering and held together again with duct tape and kindergarten paste. I write by memory, which is a beautiful liar. I write lies. I write in an alternate universe, in bed, hating the world and the word "I." I write at a desk and feel virtuous. I write without a thought in my head. I write groveling for love and attention, and indifferent to everyone and everything. I write crap, shit, clichés, whiny complaints, black speculations, goofy formulations, and give up. I go back and write *nada nada nada I suck why can't I write anything*, and give up again. I write something I like and the next day I realize it's shit. I write a poem, a story, a novel, an essay, a play. Each time I'm lost. Each time I wish I hadn't started down this road, where I can't see my hand in front of my face, a ravine on my right, a swamp on my left; there's no one else walking where I'm walking, sometimes I'm crawling, sometimes I stop and weep. Then there are stars, or a cloud shreds itself before the moon, and I get up and keep walking. Sometimes I run and there is no pleasure like running down this road in the near dark, the wind

ADDONIZIO'S CAT, EDNA ST. VINCENT MILLAY.

"I write by memory, which is a beautiful liar. I write lies. I write in an alternate universe, in bed, hating the world and the word 'I.'"

full of voices, the air alive and fluid. I write and it's finally right, the intention rhyming with the result, the marvelous unforeseen surprise of a field flowering with kisses. I write and it's good and I am queen of the kingdom and every flower is for me. I write and it's not good enough; I go and read someone who is very, very good, and feel inspired, and go back and write again. Or feel so discouraged I give up for that day, for a week, for nearly a month, until I stop believing the kingdom exists. I am cursed, until one day, mysteriously, the curse lifts. I go back to writing over and over, the irresistible lover I have known for most of my life, the monster that controls me, the jabbering creature on my back, the mother who wounds me with grace. I persist. There is a road that doesn't end until I end, and then there is another road, and another I, trying again to tell you something true.

PAM HOUSTON

For me the whole process begins with Henry James's advice: A writer should strive to be a person on whom nothing is lost. So my first task is to pay strict attention—with all of my senses—to whatever moment I am in. What I am trying to be alert to are things that have for me a kind of shimmer of resonance around them, things that, were I with a trusted friend, I would say, "Hey, look at that!" or "Did you hear that?"

"The next step is to combine this glimmer with five or ten or a hundred others . . ."

I call these writing-worthy objects and events "glimmers" when I teach, although I don't love the word glimmer because it suggests prettiness, and often these things are anything but. The word glimmer *does* correctly suggest how momentary they can be, how slight. The feeling of resonance—of recognition—that accompanies them is also often momentary and subtle, so at the same time I am paying strict attention to the world, I am also paying strict attention to my internal reaction to it.

A not particularly flashy example: Last night I gave a reading in Ketchum, Idaho, and at the rather spectacular dinner party afterward, the vodka presentation was a bottle of Ketel One frozen inside a block of ice, and inside the block of ice were frozen whole red roses. I couldn't stop looking at it, even during dinner when I had to crane my neck around to see it. Finally, I took its picture with my phone.

I have some suspicions about why the vodka bottle drew my eye: my parents were both alcoholics; vodka was their drink of choice; my mother brought on the heart attack that killed her (too young) with a combination of high-end vodka and Vioxx. There is also something in there about the bottle's beauty—it was simply stunning—which started a mini conversation in my head about art and its relationship to the things we fear most, about the healing power of beauty.

But the truth is, it is better for me to actively resist thinking about why the ice-and-rose-encrusted bottle captured my attention, so I am not in danger of over-determining the metaphor before it has had a chance to stew. The most important thing is to get the bottle down on paper, as completely and concisely and accurately as I can.

The next step is to combine this glimmer with five or ten or a hundred others, most of which, at first glance, would seem to have nothing to do with a vodka bottle, except inasmuch as they arrived on a similar warm wind of resonance. If all the ingredients of a story have this metaphorical integrity, I reason, all I have to do is get the right pieces next to each other, figure out which ones to include and exclude, let their meaning bubble up to the surface like Jack Daniels distills up out of good Tennessee mash (another parental favorite). All I have to do, in other words, is get far enough out of the story's way that I don't screw it up.

JOSH NEUFELD

I create comic books, so I write in pictures—and draw with words. I've learned over the years that the uniqueness of the comics form is the dual experience of *reading* and *seeing.*

Even though the experience of reading a comic is unified, when I create I break my creative tasks down into two distinct parts: writer and artist. Both stages use different parts of my brain, and both allow me to edit and revise the work as it moves forward. So even though my routine is regimented, I always make room for serendipity and artistic surprise.

"So even though my routine is regimented, I always make room for serendipity and artistic surprise."

I begin by writing out the story in prose form, always with the goal of showing as much as possible through action and dialogue. I then break down the text into the key moments of narration that will become the individual comics panels. The final script includes short descriptive sentences of what's going on in each panel—clues and directions to my artist self—and all character dialogue, narration or "voiceover" captions, and sound effects. It reads much like a screenplay.

Once the script is done, I step away from the computer and move to the drawing table. (Although much of my work has first appeared on the Internet, I'm old-fashioned in the sense that I draw entirely by hand.) I lay out the script, breaking it down into thumbnail sketches, using minimal detail, just enough to block out word balloon and character placement. Through thumbnailing, I assess the story's pace, check its momentum, and see how it flows from panel to panel and page to page. During this stage, I often find ways to condense elements or, conversely, to flesh out certain scenes.

Next comes penciling, the most time-intensive part of the comics-making process. That's when I scale up my thumbnails to full-size, drawing in the panel borders, characters, backgrounds, and lettering elements on tabloid-size paper. Again, when translating the layouts to this larger size, I often find better artistic or storytelling solutions. On a good day, I can pencil an entire detailed page from start to finish.

Inking is the most fun part of the process for me. It's when the story finally comes into complete focus, as I shape the pencils into finished art, often taking *away* lines more than anything else. I love the physical act of inking: the gentle pressure of the brush on the page, and the endless tiny aesthetic choices that go into each stroke. In the end, the art looks pretty much the way it will appear on the printed page.

Not every cartoonist works the way I do; many have a much looser system, and some create their work completely organically, literally writing and drawing the story at the same time. And sometimes I too find ways to skip steps along the way. But this "two-headed monster" approach works for me and helps me break down into manageable steps what can often seem a daunting task—translating the ineffable images in my head into distinct visual form.

KATHARINE RAUK

When I was younger, I had the luxury to wait for poetic inspiration to strike. I took strolls along the canal and counted the turtles. I sat on my terrace with a beer and listened to crickets at dusk. I stared out my window on Thursday afternoons, content to let my mind play in the leaves even if the page before me was blank.

These days, I am the mother of two children under three years of age, and I teach part-time at a local community college. Sometimes I am hard-pressed to brush my teeth before noon, let alone clear a path for The Muse across the living-room floor. And when I finally do find some time to myself—usually during my children's fleeting afternoon naps or after they've gone to bed—I don't feel inspired anyway. Consequently, I've had to learn how to jump-start my poems with various props and stunts. One standby is to open a nearby poetry book, snag an intriguing title from the table of contents, and begin there with my own poem of the same name. Ditto to stealing the first lines of another poet's poems. I also collect prompts sent to me by friends: write a poem about dessert, for example, or a surrealistic prose poem under a hundred words. In the past I would have turned up my nose at such dos-

"An image that makes my heart fall off its shelf, in that eerie slip from one word—or one world—to another."

es of synthetic inspiration, but I no longer get to be picky.

I'll admit I've written some awfully stale poetry this way, deciding at the end of the day that it would have been better for all concerned if I had simply taken a nap. However, I've also learned to trust the act of writing itself. "Writing is a process of discovery," I've always pronounced to my students, but I never quite believed it so full-heartedly as I do now. The prompt is a way in; it hooks me into the hairy flank of language so that I am carried, like a burr on some great elk, out beyond the margins of what I thought I could possibly say. And for me, a poem happens in this territory of the unknown: in an unexpected line break, in an image that makes my heart fall off its shelf, in that eerie slip from one word—or one world—to another. On good days, and I'm never quite sure in advance which days those will be, the scaffolding of the prompt gets smashed, and I suddenly notice an army of ants furiously building shipyards under my feet.

I still chafe against the feeling that there's never enough time and that maybe, as I am reading *Curious George* aloud to my daughter once again, a poem is slipping along the edge of the garden and will never return. But I've learned, as Dylan Thomas says in one of my favorite poems, to "[sing] in my chains like the sea." And what chains they are!—to be a mother, to be a teacher, to be a human bound in time and married to this messy world. What else to do but sing?

MATT BELL

What I need to write is the voice, but I never find an entire voice at once. Because I have to start somewhere, I'll settle: for a sound, a single sentence, an utterance in the dark, anything that has a little bit of spark or sizzle, that lights me up. This is sentence as light-bringer: There was a blank and now there is a single mote floating in the void, all potential, waiting for the bang.

> "It's okay to be wrong a lot of the time while drafting, while I'm still alone in the little room where I do my work."

Huh, I think. What's next?

Next the voice speaks again. Sometimes it speaks on its own, but more often I have to prod it, have to drag from that sentence a next one that somehow continues whatever power the first one contained. I get this part wrong a lot. Maybe most of the time. If I can see how it's wrong right away then I try again. It's okay to be wrong a lot of the time while drafting, while I'm still alone in the little room where I do my work. Plus, I can always return and revise and rewrite. I can and I will. This is how we hide our failings.

Now the voice speaks again, speaks directly or at a slant or else it reverses itself completely, and wherever it goes I need to follow its path. Then there are three sentences and then there are four and then five, six, seven, on and on. And from this process everything else I need appears, not planned but discovered, emergent: character, motivation, conflict, tension, plot, a world.

I believe that it's possible to do this from one end of a book to the other without break or fail, but that does not mean I believe it will happen for me. I'm afflicted with various kinds of personal weaknesses, lacks, and distractions that probably make this an impossible ideal. But I sometimes get a couple good sentences in a row, and if I can't figure out how to keep going then I start a new thread, build a new fragment, eventually creating a pile of these similar-voiced fragments, scenes and parts of scenes and runs of images or actions. When it feels like I have enough I start arranging the fragments, looking for patterns and possibilities—and then I write into the spaces between, trying to take advantage of juxtapositions, connections, surprises and seeming inevitabilities, places to start from again.

If this works out long enough I might get a story drafted. If it works out for a very long time, then I might be writing a novel. Whatever it turns out to be it'll be something I never could have planned—discovered one sentence at a time, arranged toward completeness, ready to be revised and rewritten mercilessly—hopefully on its way to at last becoming a manifestation of that possible world I sensed, way back on the first day, when all I had to work with was the microcosm of the whole hidden within the very first words.

Greeting Cards

Kelly Clancy

Congratulations
on your successful
Miltary Campaign

Now that you're a
CEO

On the eve of your
Ascension
to the
Throne

It's your
Golden Jubilee

Barbarians

Charles Harper Webb

"... what shall become of us without barbarians?"
—C.P. Cavafy

Lank-haired, logger-bearded, Josh and I shove
                into Sudsucker's Pub like hungry bears
down from the hills. Normally, we'd shun
    this den of cooler dudes than we.
But we've lived two weeks in Canadian woods—

slept in my truck, wolfed fresh-caught
                Kamloops trout, Life cereal, Wonder Bread,
speaking, for laughs, like Conan the Barbarian:
    swearing by Crom, who metes out dooms
from his great mountain—who hates weaklings,

and gives his people only courage, plus
                the strength and will to kill their enemies.
We've done our biz under towering evergreens,
    ransacked an old fishing lodge, and seized
what pleased us, leaving the rest to rot and feed

the fragrant pines. Now, feeling tall
                and hard as pines, we scorn these frat boys
and yuppies hot to bed the coeds,

secretaries, and receptionists who sip Slow,
Comfortable Screws Against the Wall,

and try to think they're living high.
Two beauties—Blonde and Brunette—do
the coo-and-tease with polo-shirted frat guys:
a freckled redhead; a dark-haired pretty-boy.
"By Crom," I say, catching the blonde's eye,

"you're a bright fish in white water." "True,"
says Josh. "And you"—the brunette—
"bear twin mountains fetchingly." "Who
are you assholes talking to?" snarls Pretty Boy.
"A miracle," I say. "The dumb shall speak."

I can't believe we're doing this; but
after weeks of practice, words flow easily.
"Tell me," Josh asks Red. "What is best in life?"
"What the fuck?" he replies. "The fuck
is good," Josh says. "Best, though, is to crush

your enemies, see them driven before you,
and hear the wails of their women."
"Hear that shit?" Pretty Boy asks Red.
"You fags best boogie while you can,"
Red sneers, then pushes Josh. I raise my hand.

"Stay," I command. "Let's step outside and see
whose deeds shine mightiest." "They're crazy,"

the blonde says, and shoots a scorching look.
    "No sweat," Red says, flexing his fists.
"We'll clean their clocks. Be back before

you can say *shit*." "They'll clean our cocks,"
        Josh calls, "before they eat our shit."
Outside, we're wrapped in Stygian mist.
    "Sorry, guys," Josh begins, "I don't know what
got into me," then crotch-kicks Pretty Boy,

who drops and writhes. My kick—astonishing
        to me as to Red—barely clips his hip.
He staggers. I scream, and swinging war-ax fists,
    rain on him my rage at cities that kill
wilderness—at mobs that trample fish,

animals, birds—at lawyers, politicians,
        brokers, bureaucrats who prate, *remit,*
accrue, abate, comply—the rich, popular,
    lucky, whom I see, clear as a hawk
in mountain sky, will always lord it over me.

"Let's go! Let's go!" Josh yanks me off of Red,
        then runs. My frenzy drops like a swiped coat.
"Cops could come," I think, and—Jekyll
    breaking free from Hyde—hammer for home.
When, in a week, I start my first job—teaching

eighth-grade history—my hair will be short;
                    my knuckles, healed. Tonight, I slink
toward sleep while Crom the Merciless, who scorns
      all prayers, does not attack from his mountain—
just spits my way, and turns his muscled back.

Fear Factor

Charles Harper Webb

The woman knows she's smashing
in her orange bikini, bottoms flashing half
a red dragon tattoo. Her almost-fiancé
("We're committed *now!*") flashes confidence
from steel-blue eyes hard as his pecs.
His blonde hair lights a class-president grin.

How long will he need, he's asked, to dive
into the icy pool, swim to the locked, fully
submerged cage where his love will be
freezing, holding her breath, and set her
free? "Twenty seconds max. I'm
confident." She—waving from her cage—

swells with her own confidence, which shrinks
as water shocks her toes, then turns to terror
as the shot ogles her down. Sir Commitment
plunges (*Spwak!*), flounders down to her cage,
and pokes the first of his two keys. Trapped
behind pink goggles, her eyes plead.

He jabs the second key. When *that* won't work,
his confidence shreds like Kleenex
in a blender. He's betrayed—can't breathe,

heart clanging alarm. To hell with her!
He shoots straight up as she gives the rescue
divers a crazed, throat-slashing *I quit.*

Shivering on camera, the couple try
No problem; it's just TV, holding their smiles
the way burned men hold on
their skin. Hand in hand, they churn
away. Then, not quite out of camera range,
she turns.

Be The Pack Leader

Charles Harper Webb

cries the book my wife assigned to help my "relationship"
        with our dog, Jasmine—i.e., to make her obey, but not to pee
when she sees me (which, my wife says, means she's scared).

        Is that so bad? Machiavelli thought it better for a leader
to be feared than loved (though feared *and* loved was best).
        But I don't *want* to lead. That's why I never ran

for president of anything. That, and suspecting I'd lose.
        Too bad doing what I want goose-steps hand in hand
with telling others what to do. My Cub Scout leader,

        Mr. Bimpfelberg—in khaki shorts and more ribbons
than a commissar—could barely lead our troop in singing,
        "Oh I had a little chicken / but she wouldn't lay an egg . . ."

He never showed us how to scalp an enemy, spear a moose,
        hold off the U.S. Army with bows and arrows,
or even shoot a bb gun (which, anyway, Mom wouldn't

        let me have). Still, when I'm tempted to ridicule
life's Bimpfelbergs, or—right now—my son's Little League coach,
        who knows less baseball than I know dentistry

(for which, mostly by brushing my teeth, I "earned"
        a merit badge), I remind myself, *I* could have volunteered.

But no, it's tough enough teaching *my* boy to bunt and not to cry

when he strikes out. How could I lead twelve kids who lack
my DNA? I'd forget who's up to bat, and couldn't bring myself
to yell, "Good try!" when the pitcher, attempting

to throw, blacks his own eye. Years ago, as I boiled in eighth-grade
angst, the Shangri-Las' "Leader of the Pack"
gave me hope that, if I led a pack of bikers, Sherry Ames

might not equate me with that jock strap
always kicking down the halls. The song, with its motorcycle
revving, singers wailing, "No, no, no, no, / no, no, no!"

as the leader roared into his fatal skid, made pack-leading
sound gloriously doomed. But even Dad nixed
a motorbike for me: "I don't want to scrape you off three

hundred yards of blacktop with a hoe." He earned my fear
and love the time he saved me from Foley's security.
"If you *ever* shoplift again," he raged when we got home,

"I'll knock you through the wall." Thanks to him,
I can play dictator to my kids (though not, I hope,
the Auschwitz / Gulag kind). After I'd vowed to treat my first-

ever Freshman Comp class as "fellow learners,"
then learned they wouldn't let their fellow learner speak,
I slammed our text to the floor with an atomic BLAM!

"I'll flunk you all and ruin your lives," I roared,
"if you don't shape up NOW!" These days,
I start off Stalinesque, then relax. Result: great student evals,

and no thrown books. Clearly, people want strong leaders.
Still, it's hard to believe that dogs *like* being bossed,
and are glad just to be part of the pack, which is why,

on seeing someone in the family—even our four-year-old—
Jasmine flattens her hindquarters on the floor and drags
forward like a paraplegic before bellying up, frog-

kicking her legs until we pat her and coo, "Good girl."
I've bought the democracy ideal so completely, I feel bad
reading the (probably *mojado*) gardeners the riot act

as my Armenian neighbor does so cheerfully.
Raised in the USSR, he hates the "asshole leaders"
we elect. "This is best we have?" he demands, although—

a U.S. citizen for years—he knows our campaigns
favor the corrupt, hypocritical, power-mad.
I've read that medieval peasants were proud to serve

their "God-given" lord—that untouchables accepted
the caste system as just and right—that some slaves
in the U.S. embraced their lot. Can that be true?

Woody Allen says people will follow any order, however
asinine, if it comes from a deep, well-modulated voice.
When I talk to Jasmine, that's how I make mine.

NORTH
WAS
MY
HOME

Libration

Jenni Moody

The house is cool. Quiet. Calm. Billie leaves the door open behind her, ready to run out again if her dad is awake. She can make out the shape of the furniture, but the details are blurry without her glasses. She knows enough from memory to step out of the way of the coffee table, around the squeaking floorboards, to put her hand out to tell her body just where the sofa reaches.

Upstairs her sister, Jean, is fast asleep with her stuffed animals. The night-light in her room a faint and tiny star. She couldn't have slept through all of the yelling. Not Jean who calls out into the hallway every time Billie comes in late at night from a party. Jean with her child's smile. The one Billie is here to save.

She pauses at the bottom of the stairs, listening. The summer crickets are at their loudest. A car passes. The headlights sweep around the room, and when they hit her face she ducks away. Her hand grips the smooth knob of the stair railing. Her bare feet arched against the hardwood floor, ready to run.

☆

The planetarium is slightly dingy. Spider webs hang between the Styrofoam planets in a display case. An old woman sits behind a counter by the door. She takes a long time to count back the change from the twenty dollar bill that Jean's father gave for admission.

There's a group of schoolchildren sitting in the best seats. They're a year older than Jean, and from a different school. They all wear matching shirts that say Chesterfield Academy. The private school. The kids have a map of the moon taped to clipboards. Their small hands hold pencils with spoons taped to the top so that they won't be accidentally stolen. One boy smiles at Jean, and she turns her body so that her father cannot see her wave back.

She has a marble and a rubberband and a small plastic pony with purple hair in the pocket of her dress, but she doesn't take them out to play with them. Billie warned her not to fidget. But Billie isn't here with them. She's gone out to a party, and their dad was pretty mad about it. The rubberband stretches, pops, stretches between her thumb and middle finger, hidden in the soft pocket of her hand-me-down dress.

Jean and her father sit together on one of the old benches. She counts the number of people there. Just under twenty. Across from her there are some men. When Jean goes back up to the counter to pick up a free star chart she passes them, the smoke of campfire lingering in their clothes.

"Did you skin it yourself?"

A man with a bright orange hunter's cap spits a dark liquid into his soda bottle. "Yeah. Hung her up in the back yard."

Jean sits down again beside her father and spreads the star chart across her lap. She can hear every word they say, as if they had cupped their hands up to her ear.

"What about the foal?"

The man's bottom lip is puffed out with chewing tobacco. It makes his words muffled and heavy. "I'll get her next season."

It is a game she and her father play. They sit across the room from some people who are obvious newbies, and they don't speak for the first few minutes. They listen to the people on the other side of the planetarium, to find out what secrets people reveal when they think no one is listening.

☆

Billie's hand sweats. She wipes it on her pajama bottoms. Her dry throat aches, her mind fizzing a bit at the edges. But she doesn't have time to get some water. He could wake up any moment. She takes one step onto the stairs. She waits. She listens. Glass shifts in the garbage can in the kitchen and makes a clink. She thinks she knows the type of glass by the heavy smell in the room. Dark green bottles with thick bottoms, the rim stained red with wine.

"They listen to the people on the other side of the planetarium, to find out what secrets people reveal when they think no one is listening."

But they were at the planetarium until at least 9 p.m. That's how late they ran when Billie was a kid. He must have started drinking right when they got home.

A high whine and water running through the pipes stops her. He must be awake. She runs back to the front door, bumping into the sofa along the way. It grunts as its wooden feet scoot across the hardwood floor. She crouches down on the front step and puts her head between her knees. Counting her breathing, measuring it, congratulating each slow exhale.

Her red Mustang sits by the front curb. There's a streak of white on the front bumper. Her mother's the one who put it there.

Billie considers running up to one of the doors, ringing the doorbell, and asking the person to call the police. All along the quiet street the front porch lights stay off. No windows lit by lamps or the blue glow of television. It's 3 a.m. on a Saturday. This is a gated community, a place where engineers and businessmen and even an astronaut have come to retire. People who have paid to not be part of these kinds of situations. Billie wonders if the police would just throw her out of the gates to the community.

Her breathing steadies.

"I'll just be in there for a minute," she thinks.

She stands up and steps back into the house. Her hand lingers on the front door, making sure it will stay open when she lets go.

Jean.

The keys. Her glasses. Her phone.

She walks into her father's house silently, feeling for the first time like a thief, even though it is a name he has called her before.

☆

"You little thief."

Jean holds the glossy star chart on her lap. She picked it up from the table by the front door. But she hadn't stolen it. The lady behind the counter had nodded to her, told her it was alright to take it back to her seat. She looks up at her father, wondering if he is making a joke.

"Put it back."

His voice is not unkind. But it is stern, and Jean does not argue. She travels the stars one last time, her fingers rubbing over the small, glow-in-the-dark paint that traces the constellations. She hopes that it will rub off on her fingers.

She folds the map together. Spoons and bears and sisters all bending into each other.

Maybe Billie has an old star map she doesn't want now that she's older.

The lady at the desk gives Jean a smile and presses a sticker onto her t-shirt before she can protest. It is a star. Jean sits beside her father, swinging her feet, hoping that when the lights go off her star will be visible.

☆

Billie makes it to the top of the stairs without too much noise. She peeks around the corner, and the door to her father's bedroom is shut. Her hand rests on her throat, as if it could shield her windpipe. There has been no time yet for mirrors, but by the ache of her skin she will have to wear a scarf around her neck to her classes tomorrow. Not an hour ago his hands were on her neck, his rage filled the house.

Just like your mother. Sneaking in late at night.

The hallway floor is full of squeaking boards, all the way down to her bedroom at the far end. She steps and the floor groans, as if tired of all of this late night moving about.

Billie waits in the hallway, ready to run down the stairs and out of the house forever. She's waiting for the sound of the door unlatching, for his stumbling forward with his fists against the wall. But his door stays shut.

"Billie waits in the hallway, ready to run down the stairs and out of the house forever."

And so does the one with the glow-in-the-dark star sticker on the doorknob.

☆

The show starts. The lights dim slowly, a rapid dusk falling. On the dome the stars appear. Only a few at first, but then more and more step out of the dark. Stars that can't be seen from the city. A woman gives a tour of the constellations with a laser pointer. Beginning at the North Star, she works her way around the sky, using the red beam to draw the swoop of a bear's back and the belt hanging from Orion's hips.

When the sky has been mapped out, the slideshow begins, and the woman guides her audience across the moon. The kids with the clipboards stare in awe, and then scribble on their maps as the woman names the seas. Jean pulls the head of her plastic pony out of her pocket to take a peek at the slideshow.

Jean thinks of the moon as an emotional journey. Maybe in the future there will be a tour you can take through all of the romantically named areas.

The Ocean of Storms, where you face your fears.

From there into the Sea of Vapors, where the past comes to settle its score.

And then into the Sea of Serenity, and finally the Lake of Sleep.

★

Billie's father does not wake up.

She steps into her bedroom and stands in the dark.

Broken glass lies scattered across the floor. She leans into the room and picks up her shoes. She shakes them to make sure there are no slivers of glass inside and runs her hand into the toes to be sure. Then she slips them on and steps into the room.

Her glasses have fallen onto the floor, but they are not broken. She puts them on and looks around, measuring what she can and cannot take.

There's a sound in her closet. A soft knock. Billie steps into the closet, presses her ear against the wall. Knock knock knock.

It's Jean in her bedroom. They haven't talked to each other through the walls like this since before their mother left. Back when the fighting between their parents was so bad that they couldn't risk running through the hallway to the other's room.

They don't have a code. The knocks don't correspond to letters of the alphabet or phrases. But because they are sisters, they know what the knocks mean.

I'm here. I'm okay. Are you there?

Billie listens to Jean's raps on the wall, the knuckles of her first two fingers readying a reply.

☆

The children in the planetarium begin to pick on each other. They shift in their seats, hitting one another on the head with their pencils. The woman with the laser pointer tells the tech guy to bring up the lights, and she places a tin cooking pan on the floor.

"I'll need some volunteers," she says.

Jean jumps to her feet. There's a tug at the back of her t-shirt, pulling her back down onto the seat. Her father lets go of her t-shirt and gives her head a pat.

The children race to the woman, and she hands them each a rock. They stand over the cooking pan and one by one drop their rock. On impact, white strands of flour bounce out and stretch across the top layer of brown cinnamon. Jean listens to the soft sounds of impact. The thuds sound like heavy footfalls. The woman calls these rays of debris ejecta. A teenage girl slumps over in a fit of giggles, and her friend smiles beside her, her cheeks reddening. The woman only has a few rocks left. The children begin to fight over who can drop them into the pan.

The woman holds the rocks out to Jean. "Why don't we let someone else have a try?"

Her father swipes at the back of her shirt, but Jean sprints forward to clutch at the rocks. She's careful not to look back at her father's eyes as she raises her hand and lets the first rock fall. But the pebble only makes a small spray. She tries again, raising her hand high above her head and letting another rock go. A puff of white flour flies across the pan. But it isn't enough. The last rock Jean throws. It bounces off of the corner of the pan with a twang, the rock flying into a faraway corner.

"Jean wraps her tiny arms around Billie's neck. 'Don't go.'"

Jean runs back to her seat as the adults in the audience laugh. She draws her feet up to her chest, tucks her head in between her arms. She wishes Billie were here to tell her it's all right. To make everybody else be quiet.

Beside Jean her father laughs in deep, thunderous roars.

☆

It is hard to walk away. She picks up her backpack full of college textbooks. She opens a duffel bag and begins to stuff clothing in it, hangers and all. There's a laundry bag in the closet from her brief stay in the dorm before her father stopped paying. She opens the bag and begins to fill it with shoes, jewelry, hats, stuffed animals.

Billie shoves her phone and her car keys in her purse, and then lifts the shoulder strap over her head. Everything else she can leave behind.

She turns to look around the room. Jean stands in the doorway, her stuffed rabbit in the crook of her arm, covered to her toes in her Disney princess nightgown. Billie shoulders her backpack, swings her purse over to the side so she has room to run, and picks up Jean.

Jean wraps her tiny arms around Billie's neck. "Don't go."

Billie walks down the hallway, into Jean's room. She picks up Jean's school backpack and throws clothes inside. Jean's forehead is warm against her neck, and she remembers holding Jean when she was a baby. When their mother stopped getting up at night to feed her. Reading stories about sailing away from monsters in an enchanted boat, and swearing not to step onto that boat without her little sister.

Jean stretches out her arms, sleepwalking through their morning routine of putting on her backpack. Billie stands in the doorway with Jean balanced on her hip. Three. Two. One.

Ready.

Run.

✯

The lecturer tells everyone to give the kids a big round of applause, then the kids are sent back to their seats.

One of the men across from Jean raises his hand. The lecturer points at him, and he leans forward.

"What about the other side of the moon? You know, the dark side?" He starts to hum some Pink Floyd.

The lecturer looks tired, like this has happened before. Or maybe it happens every weekend. But the lecturer has a strategy for dealing with these types of questions.

"Does anyone know why we only see one face of the moon?"

One of the kids sitting on the front row raises his hand.

"Because of the tides?"

The lecturer nods, smiles. And describes how the moon is tidally locked, how it does not turn in its orbit like Earth does.

The kid looks confident that this is the end of the discussion, but the lecturer asks another question.

"So how much of the moon can we see?"

The kid raises his hand again. "59 percent"

"So if we can only see one side of the moon, then why can we see 59 percent, instead of just 50 percent?"

The kid shakes his head. He hasn't gotten that far yet.

"It's because of something called libration. The moon has a slight wobble, and this allows us to see just a little bit more of the sides that are usually hidden."

The lecturer turns to the Pink Floyd guy, ready for his retort.

But he doesn't hear the kid's answer. He's too busy looking at the photograph on the projector screen of a crater called Pythagoras. A grin spreads across the man's face.

"What's that jerk so happy about?" her father whispers.

Jean sees it.

In the center of Pythagoras, there is the outline of a man. His body splayed out as if it were the chalk outline of a crime scene. Beside him lies his dog.

Jean knows the man and his dog aren't real, their images just the shadows and light giving a shape meaning. Like shapes in clouds. The face of Jesus in toasted bread.

The man across the room turns to look at Jean's father. And from the cold look in the man's eyes, Jean knows that he has heard her father's whisper.

☆

At the door to her sister's bedroom Billie listens. There's no sound in the house, no stream of light into the hallway from her father's door. She takes a deep breath.

She runs down the hallway, down the stairs, to the front door. It doesn't matter now if he wakes up.

She's almost to the front door when Jean freaks out. She struggles in Billie's arms, pushing against Billie's chest, trying to get free. When Billie holds her tighter, Jean starts screaming. She hits Billie in the neck, and Billie stumbles back, her arms opening. Jean hits the floor with a heavy thud and then runs off, up the stairs, her backpack bouncing.

"Jean!" Billie whisper-calls.

There is the sound of a bedroom door opening. The upstairs hall lamp turns on, filling the corner of the living room.

"Jean knows the man and his dog aren't real, their images just the shadows and light giving a shape meaning. Like shapes in clouds. The face of Jesus in toasted bread."

☆

Outside the planetarium, people stand staring up at the dark sky. The tech guy from the planetarium show has his personal telescope out on the grass field. He's trying to focus in on the moon, but the weather is against him. There's a line forming behind him, waiting to look through the eyepiece.

The teacher hands out ice cream to the kids from a red and white cooler. The kids try to manage eating their fudgesicles and avoid getting tagged by their classmates who have already finished eating.

The teacher tries to call the kids over to wipe off their sticky hands, but they're in full play mode. Jean and her father stand in line to look through the telescope. The tech guy has finally calibrated everything.

The kids playing tag use the line for the telescope. They weave in and out of the adults, hiding behind legs, feinting in and out of the line while being chased.

The boy who knew all of the answers during the planetarium show stands beside a tree. He smiles and beckons her over. When Jean's father leans down to look through the telescope's lens, Jean runs to the tree. She doesn't stop until she's behind it, out of sight.

☆

"Jean!"

Billie can see Jean's tiny feet poking out from the top of the stairs. If she can just get Jean to come back down they'll have enough time.

"Please Jean, please."

She moves forward. There is a crash from upstairs, the sound of the floorboards creaking.

The sound of his footsteps on the stairs freezes her.

Jean's voice is full of trust. "Dad!"

Then there is the slap of his hand against the wall, steadying himself as he comes down the stairs.

Billie runs.

She locks the car as soon as she's inside. By the time the living-room light turns on she has started the car and shifted it into drive. When he stands on the front porch, his white hair sticking up like a madman's, she is pulling away from the curb. He stands there on the front step, holding Jean in his arms.

Billie hits the steering wheel. "No!"

She wants to roll down her window, to shout at Jean to run and get in the car. But she remembers the day her mother left, and how Jean wouldn't even hug her goodbye.

There is a look in her father's eyes that she has only seen once before. As Billie drives away she looks in her rearview mirror and watches as he closes the door and turns off the front porch light.

☆

The boy hands Jean a fudgesicle. They sit together behind the giant tree. It's evening, but the moon is full and glowing. Her hands grow sticky, the thick chocolaty ice melting in little streams. The boy pulls a star chart out of his pocket—the same one that Jean's father made her put back.

He holds out the map as if to bargain. "Want to kiss?"

Jean shrugs her shoulders.

"Haven't you ever kissed anyone before?" he asks.

"No, 'cause I'm a lady."

The boy leans in and kisses her cheek before Jean can turn away. His lips are warm and sticky, and Jean rubs her cheek where he touched it. He tosses the star chart on the ground and then runs back to the group near the planetarium. There's still half of the fudgesicle left, but Jean doesn't feel like eating it anymore.

She covers the popsicle stick and the small bit of ice cream left on it with a leaf, and picks up the map. Pressed between two fingers, held at a corner, because her hands are dirty and sticky.

Her father is waiting for her.

She's afraid he will take away the star chart again, or make her give it back to the planetarium lady.

He kneels down, face to face with Jean. He pulls a tiny paper packet from his wallet and tears off one of the ends. It is one of the moist wipes that they get when they go to eat ice cream together on Sundays. The cloth from the packet is warm, and her father uses it to wipe away the stickiness of the fudgesicle on her hands, and a streak she didn't know was on her face.

Her father picks her up, and she wraps her arms around his neck. They walk past a school bus, the boy who gave her the map watching her through the window. He tries to pull the top part of the window down so he can lean out and yell something, but he presses at the latches over and over and they don't give way. Jean spreads the star map behind her father's back as he carries her to the car. In the darkness, the tiny stars begin to glow. The dirt of the forest beneath her fingernails, and the warmth of the boy's kiss still on her cheek.

The Breaking-Up Game

Liz N. Clift

Players

Game requires exactly three (3) players, at least one (1) unaware that s/he is playing. The characters are as follows:

Primary Player (The instructions are catered to you.)

Significant Other (You probably shouldn't read the directions too carefully. Spoiler alert.)

Potential Suitor (If you're reading these instructions, we can't play the game.)

Ages

Dating age and up. Ideally, you should be beyond those awkward teenage years when you went to the mall to be alone. For best results, the Primary Player and Significant Other should be considering living together in the near future.

Rules & Setup

The game starts with emotional betrayal. Make a friend who will make your Significant Other (SO) jealous, a Potential Suitor (PS). This friend need not be anything more than a potential, but if something develops, all the better for you.

Primary Player: For best results, your SO should be long distance and wildly different from you. See the following chart for examples:

You or Significant Other	**Significant Other or You**
Atheistic and/or religiously confused	Devout, evangelical Christian
Peace Corps	Military
Pro-social justice	Hates any sort of welfare
Pro-socialized medicine	Pro-private health care
Unaffiliated, left-of-center politically	Die-hard Republican
Pro-gun control	Keeps weapons in every room of the house
Pro-choice	Pro-life

You or Significant Other	Significant Other or You
Believes labels like "men's work" and "women's work" should be eradicated from the English language.	Classifies "men's work" as mowing the lawn, doing anything with hammers or wrenches, changing the oil, and repairing drywall. "Women's work" entails vacuuming, doing all things with Windex and Scrubbing Bubbles, baking, and cleaning the toilet.
Difficulty with expressing affection; shows emotion by taking care of others	Believes words are enough; verbally expresses affection frequently and is hurt when this is not reciprocated
Comfortable with silence	Uncomfortable with silence
Believes September 11, 2001, was a traumatic day in American history, but realizes almost as many people die each day of heart disease	Believes September 11, 2001, is worthy of deep remembrance and patriotism because Americans died unexpectedly, in a way we could not control

Directions

1) Your current relationship with SO should involve high emotional investment. Until recently, you would have called this person one of your best friends. Probably s/he still is.

   Note: SO – Don't worry, nothing's wrong. Just keep doing what you're doing. Move backward (mandatory) at your discretion.

2) Spend a rainy Saturday emotionally cheating on your SO with PS at a coffee shop, and later at a local park while walking your dog (walk yourselves if you do not have a dog). Tell PS things you've never trusted yourself to tell anyone.
    a. Remember, two to four weeks ago your SO asked you to share something s/he doesn't know about you.
    b. Remember, two to four weeks ago you didn't trust yourself to share. Or, more specifically, you didn't trust your SO. Really, it's the same thing, isn't it?
        i. If you choose A, do not advance forward.
        ii. If you choose B, do not advance forward.

3) Spend eight hours with PS that rainy Saturday. It's not your first time losing hours with/to this person.
    a. Realize you're in a kind of shitty relationship and both you and SO are being kind of shitty people. Advance forward at your discretion.

    Note: SO – Really, you're doing fine. There's nothing to worry about. Move backward again.

    b. Tell PS about it early in the day. S/he will not have feedback directly related to relationship. Try to gauge if there's any jealousy on PS's part.
        i. Feel better when you've made the decision to break things off with your SO. Less tired. Less stressed. Advance forward at your discretion but be prepared to move backward.

1. Realize for the first time how long you've really been turning over why the relationship is wrong — longer than you've known PS.

ii. Resolve to end things soon. But not today. It's your SO's birthday. Or it's your anniversary. Or it's just a bad idea to end things on days ending in –y.

1. Go backward one step for every reason you come up with.

4) That evening, call SO. Say Happy Birthday. Or, How was your day? Or think, I can't end this when I hear his/her voice.

a. Remember your SO has told you s/he'd never hurt you.

b. Think of all the ways it could work. Make a list of these reasons. Burn it and lose one day.

Note: SO – This might be a good time to talk about the long-term. Your SO is feeling vulnerable and anxious. Talking about the future will give him/her a sense of security. Or push him/her over the brink because s/he can't think about you in the long term. But hey, isn't it worth the gamble?

c. If applicable, remember s/he didn't want to commit to a long-distance relationship, so whatever you are, you are not dating. Even though if someone overheard your conversations they would conclude otherwise.

i. Perhaps because SO says "I love you" and you say it back. Or because you're talking about a future together. Or because you're both still being shitty people. Lose three days pondering this.

5) Lie to SO when s/he asks what you did with your day, who you were with. Do not lie out of obligation, but because you believe it's the right thing to do.
    a. You should feel like shit about lying, because you've already been lying at least five weeks. Remind yourself you haven't ended things sooner because you two have been friends for more than a decade.
        i. Hope being passive-aggressive will work before you end things. In three days. Or three weeks. Whatev.
            1. Take three steps back for being passive-aggressive.
        ii. Feel slightly guilty about lying, but only because of what PS might think. Know s/he has little tolerance for passive-aggressive behavior, because it means you're not taking control of your life, of the situation.
    b. Remember you've been lying about various things since you last saw SO, almost two months ago. Mostly about whom you've been hanging out with. You don't want to trigger the jealous side.

    Note: SO – If you're not the jealous type, it doesn't really matter. What matters is that the Primary Player believes you're the jealous type.

6) When your SO tells you s/he loves and/or misses you, respond in kind. Or almost in kind. Reciprocate. Enjoy the feeling in the pit of your stomach that tells you this is wrong. Hush that feeling. Tell yourself that it is good to feel this way. You feel this way because you know the relationship is wrong.

   a. Best done over the phone. In person, s/he might be able to read the lie in your body language.
   b. If done in person, fake the body language. Do it, damn it. You can fake anything.
      i. Like an orgasm. Or love. Or interest in something you're not interested in at all.

7) Tell your SO you're tired. This is not a lie.

8) S/he does not want to let you off that easily again. Third night in a row. Don't talk much. You're tired, after all, and wishing you were still talking to PS.
   a. Advance at your discretion.

9) SO mentions s/he doesn't like it when you're so quiet. S/he can't tell if s/he's done something to upset you, hasn't said something s/he should have, etc.

   Note: SO – Ask repeatedly if you've done something wrong. This never gets annoying.

   a. For every time you reassure your SO nothing's wrong, move backward.

10) Talk until your phone starts to die. Listen to the phone give warning beeps.
   a. Consider plugging in your phone.
      i. Decide not to. Advance forward at your discretion.

11) Allow the phone to die.

Note: SO – The next time you talk, be sure to point out how the phone always dies at the "crucial moment." Use that phrase exactly. Crucial moment.

12) Send an email to PS about things you talked about during your rainy Saturday together. Title it simply: "Thoughts."

   a. Yes, this is cliché. Go with it.
   b. Yes, you're tired. Push through and write the damn email. Lose one night.

13) Get ready for bed. Plug in your phone, but do not turn it back on.

Note: SO – This would be an opportune time to call. Maybe more than once. Leave messages. Text. Your SO won't find this annoying at all.

14) The next day:

   a. Listen to voicemail, if necessary. Your SO may have called after your phone died and suggested you call her/him back.
      i. If so, do not call back.
      ii. Instead, send a text saying you were too tired. It's not entirely a lie.
   b. Write the rules for a game about ending a relationship. Begin with a list. Lose one week.

15) Make the decision: I'll end it Tuesday. Or Wednesday. Next month. Soon.

A Conversation with Charles Simic

Chris Forhan

Charles Simic, who served as the 2007-2008 United States poet laureate, is one of the nation's most honored and distinguished poets. Born in Belgrade, Yugoslavia, in 1938, he emigrated to the U.S. in 1954. Over the last few decades, he has published dozens of books of poetry and prose, including Selected Poems: 1963-1983, The Voice at 3:00 AM: Selected Late and New Poems, The World Doesn't End, *which received the Pulitzer Prize for Poetry, and, this year, his most recent volume,* New and Selected Poems: 1963-2012. *Simic has been prolific not just as a poet but also as an editor, translator, and reviewer, and he has received numerous awards, including Guggenheim, National Endowment for the Arts, and MacArthur fellowships, the Wallace Stevens Award, and, in 2011, the Robert Frost Medal from the Poetry Society of America for distinguished lifetime service to American poetry. He lives in Strafford, New Hampshire, and is emeritus professor of English at the University of New Hampshire. This conversation with Butler associate professor of English Chris Forhan took place before a group of Butler students in April 2009 and was continued through email correspondence.*

You were born in 1938 in Yugoslavia, and you've often written and talked about how in your first few years, in Belgrade, you were bombed by both the Axis and Allied powers and were familiar with broken glass and burned-out buildings and the uniforms of dead German soldiers. It was quite an upbringing. Eventually you and your family immigrated to America—you have said that Stalin and Hitler were your travel agents. All of that has necessarily informed your sensibility. I wonder, as we have moved into this new century of wars, how those initial experiences affect your understanding of what is going on in the world today.

Very much so. When a city is bombed, it's mostly innocents who get killed. Now we talk about precision bombing, and they're probably a bit more accurate in hitting what they aim to hit. But a lot of the time, as we see in Afghanistan, it's civilians who get it. And so when I see a city being bombed, I can imagine what's going on on the ground.

Is it foolish to think that humanity might be improving in any fashion in regard to this, or are the weapons just getting more precise?

No, I don't think humanity is improving. I mean, you still have the same kind of carnage even today, not as indiscriminate—I mean, the second World War was really incredibly cruel if you think of the carpet-bombing of German cities, the fire-bombing of Japanese cities. They just didn't care. Their intention was to kill a lot of civilians. I don't think that's true today, but innocents and bystanders still suffer.

When you first came to the United States, you moved first to New York and then to Chicago, and you went to high school in Oak Park, where Hemingway went to high school, and you started writing poems. If my math is correct, this is the fiftieth anniversary of the first publication of your poems, in The Chicago Review.

Yeah, it was the winter issue of 1959. It came out, I believe, in late December of 1958.

Fifty years. Does that number make any sense to you?

No. I'm glad you reminded me, since I don't think about such things. The two poems that came out I have never reprinted. I think I looked at them maybe thirty years ago and realized they were not very good. It was wonderful to have poems accepted, but it's hard for me to imagine today what the editors saw in them.

Does that mean you were sending out your work too early?

Oh, yeah, sure, I was sending my work out too early. When you're young, you don't grasp how badly you write. I remember sending poems to *Poetry* magazine in Chicago, and they came back within a week. Of course, it was Chicago, so it wasn't very far—but I was very surprised that there was not even a printed rejection slip.

That's the way it was for me. I had no idea. I was writing poems and didn't know if they were any good, and I didn't know anybody who could tell me, so I sent them to magazines, and they were rejected, and I realized, well, they're no good.

> "When you're young, you don't grasp how badly you write. I remember sending poems to *Poetry* magazine in Chicago, and they came back within a week."

Yeah.

As I read your work, these are images, or objects, that appear again and again: dusty storefronts, pawnshops, fortune tellers, birds—caged or otherwise, maimed dogs and black cats, dolls—perhaps headless or stuck with pins, lipsticked lips, mirrors, broken windows, world-weary grandmothers, mysterious waiters, threadbare coats, dust, and rain. That's almost a comprehensive list. There are more. My question is, do you have any sense of why these things keep bubbling up into your poetic consciousness?

Well, they're all things that I have a great deal of interest in. Something like dusty pawnshop windows: It's not often that you can see a pawnshop today, but if you lived in New York or Chicago in those days, in the '50s, there were pawnshops on the Lower East Side in New York, a few per block. I always liked windows, store windows, but pawnshops have the best. All sorts of interesting things—musical instruments, radios, steak knives, a kid's pair of roller skates—and you're thinking: "Some poor kid's parents pawned them." You always have the impression that each one of these objects has a story to tell. All you have to do is look long enough and you'll begin to hear the story behind the object. They're also aesthetically interesting, just the way they look, thrown together, without rhyme or reason by the owner of the shop.

Broken windows—I saw a lot of broken windows in my life because of the bombings. I think the thing about dolls, too, that also is a wartime memory. There were a lot of ruins of buildings that were bombed, and I played in some of them with my friends. It was terrific climbing up and down. And, you know, you see a doll and it makes an impression.

I forget what else you mentioned . . .

We can go through them one at a time if you want . . .

Don't. But mention another one.

Well, how about the waiters? You have really strange waiters in your poems.

Waiters, yeah. Well, I always had an interest in waiters. I spent a lot of time in restaurants, bars, and these waiters that I describe are not precisely the kind of waiters you encounter today, or at least less so, but old-time waiters—you had that job probably for life. I remember an old Polish restaurant where the waiters had to wear tuxedoes, and these tuxedoes were one hundred years old, and the waiters all walked slowly, taking forever to get from the kitchen to your table. You'd order a lobster—I didn't, but somebody I knew once did—and they brought lobster with sauerkraut.

Sauerkraut goes with everything.

Exactly. But looking at these waiters—there's something very theatrical about them. They were like characters in a play one walked into the middle of.

Your description of the pawnshop windows and the collection of odds and ends in them reminds me of your interest in Joseph Cornell's work. He has these boxes in which he's collected various things from all around the city and found this unique arrangement of objects that originally didn't seem to belong together. I'm not sure how to formulate this question, but I'll give it a shot. Your poems are oftentimes like that for me: a collection of disparate details, and they start talking to each other. You've written a lot about chance as a force in our lives and in art, and sometimes I read your poems, and it seems that the idea is that any given moment or collection of experiences or objects is unique—it's there and it's gone, and it's marvelous, or horrifying, or whatever. But it doesn't necessarily mean anything beyond itself. Then there are times when it seems you have this hunch they might mean something beyond themselves; in other words, there may be some kind of transcendent reality that underpins all of this, and your trees are often seemingly whispering about this big secret. So, which is it? Is there a transcendent truth, or do we exist amid a random collection of things and it is foolish to infer something larger from them?

There are two questions here. The first question was about Cornell. Joseph Cornell was an American artist who spent most of his life roaming the streets of New York City and peeking into junk shops, dime stores, and used bookstores and so forth and collecting things that no one else would collect, odd objects, programs for old concerts, movie posters, just all sorts of odd and strange things which he then incorporated in his art. He would have little wooden boxes, and inside the box he would put two or three of these objects—arrange them in a way that seemed pleasing to him and certainly is pleasing to us. But it was all done in a very strange way. He would find something interesting, like some little marble, a kid's marble, and some other kind of little thing, and he had a box all ready for it, and he'd feel in New York City there are three or four other little things like that—odd, found things—that would fit with this. But he didn't know where they were or what they were. And he would make his daily trips into the city—he lived in Queens and went to the city and just kind of poked around. And, of course, his house, his basement, was just full of junk. Everybody else would think it was trash he was collecting because these were not valuable things; these were things that a normal person would throw out. But he was in love with them. He used to call them "his loot." He'd go over them the way a miser goes over his hoard of gold, and then put one of them aside and look at it, and look at it, and finally place it in one of the empty wooden boxes he used as a kind of frame. And then he'd find another one that he felt went with the first. And when they were together, he suffered over their position, over how they were placed. He'd move them just a little this way and then that way. I didn't know about him when I was in love with pawnshops, but once I read about Cornell, I realized this is the way I work, too, putting words and images together, waiting for them to fit in a kind of collage, a combination of deliberation and accident.

"We look at the world both with eyes closed and with eyes open."

As far as transcendence, and what the trees are whispering, someone told me recently after a reading that I have too many poems about trees. You've been to my house. I live surrounded by woods, so—

What are you going to do?

Yeah, what can I do?

Not everybody's trees whisper things to them.

Well, trees are always talking. Read Robert Frost. He's got a lot of poems about trees rustling, the leaves carrying on like they were talking. But as far as transcendence goes, that's a very complicated question. Is it simply a feeling that there is another world, another reality out beyond what we see and hear? I don't think I ever quite say there is another world beyond the visible in my poems, but I tend to agree with the trees that one ought to worry and think about that possibility.

I'm reminded of a very early poem of yours, "Evening," in which you write, "The snail gives off stillness. / The weed is blessed." This feels of its time . . .

Those early poems were very much in that tradition of the Transcendentalists. I was reading Roethke a lot and James Wright, too, so it wasn't so much my own experience, but my experience colored by literature. Once I became my own poet, I was less willing to say things like that.

From the beginning, your images have been striking. In a notebook entry, you write, "'He has great images,' we used to say, and we meant that the poet kept surprising us by his wild associations. Total freedom of the imagination was our ideal then. That's all we loved and demanded from the poetry we were going to write." Is this still true? Or do you love and demand other things, too, from your poems and the poems of others?

Not true anymore. Now I want the whole poem to be memorable.

Your poems emphasize, on one hand, the dream-like and surreal and, on the other, the literal—including both moments of simple domestic joy and war and suffering. What is the relationship between these two modes of expression, or have I created a false dichotomy?

We look at the world both with eyes closed and with eyes open. I can't conceive leaving my memories and my imagination out, nor can I conceive not paying attention to what goes on around me. They can be seen as two points of view.

Is there a moral component to—or consequence of—great images or good poetry—or only an aesthetic or imaginative one?

Only if one thinks of morality as a form of integrity. Things well made, be they pieces of furniture or poems, have a moral component in that sense.

You tend to be a minimalist; you write short poems—

Sure.

And there's something Louise Glück says—she's very interested in things that are unfinished, the elliptical nature of a lot of art—and she says, "What is wanted in art is to harness the power of the unfinished." Does that make sense to you as an aesthetic?

It makes sense to me. You know, "less is more" is the old saying about poetry—because poems are really collaborations between the reader and the poet. You read a haiku. If it works and engages your imagination, you fill in all the things left out. And if nothing happens, that's it; it's the end of it. You turn the page. That has always amazed me: how you can bring to life something so brief. There is a haiku which I read, like, twenty or thirty years ago and I still remember it. I've no idea who wrote it, but the guy gets out of bed in the morning on his dead wife's side and steps with his bare foot on her comb lying next to the bed. As a reader you shudder and begin to imagine that bare foot stepping on a comb of the dead wife with perhaps her hairs still sticking out of it. So the power of something small—and, as Louise says, unfinished—can have immense power. Cold morning, cold foot, cold comb—I wonder what their marriage must have been like? If you give the reader something like that, then they'll never forget the poem.

At the same time—and, granted, you've never written an epic as far as I know; you don't have a Paradise Lost *in a drawer somewhere—some of the poems of yours that I appreciate the most are a little looser-limbed. I was happy that you read "Shelley" last night; I like those "being a young guy in New York" poems: "Shelley," "St. Thomas Aquinas," and "The Initiate." And then there is a different kind of poem but, again, a longer poem, "White"—*

A series of lyrics, yes—

—which feels to me central in your work. Do you see those longer poems, either those two- or three-page narrative poems or "White," as being somehow anomalous for you, or are they all part of the same project as your other poems?

I like them both very much. One of the problems with something short, very brief, is that you get obsessed to encompass everything in a few words and end up writing the same poem over and over again. You become predictable. My tendency has been, even with things that are longer, to cut down. I've very often written poems the length of "Shelley" or "Aquinas," and then looking at them realized that a passage of ten or twelve lines was the heart of the whole thing.

Speaking of predictable—and I don't mean to be critical at all—but, reading your most recent book, That Little Something, *I notice a pattern. There's a continual sense of the speaker of the poems, the consciousness of the poems, being in an in-between state, on the way to some place or having just left some place—caught in time or something. These are the endings of the first four poems of the book:*

> I've no return ticket
> To wherever it is I came from
>   earlier this evening.

. . . you hurry to some appointment
Where you are now certain to arrive late.

. . . you,
All frazzled and descending in a hurry.

I better get the passkey and see for myself.
I better bring along a book of matches too.

This reminds me of one of my favorite poems of yours, an earlier poem, "Furniture Mover," in which, in my reading of the poem, anyway, this furniture mover is maybe time itself or whatever is this thing just beyond our grasp that holds everything together, and the speaker of the poem desires for once to be ahead of the furniture mover and meet him at his destination, ahead of time. Is there some sort of obsession or philosophy, or at least interest, of yours that accounts for these poems? Or am I reading too much into it?

No. I think it's interesting what you say, that I'm always in transit. It most likely has something to do with my life because I've certainly moved around a great deal. When I was a kid in Yugoslavia, it never occurred to me that I would ever leave the street where I was born. It never occurred to my parents either. They were the kind of people who just stayed where they were born, in the same place, in the same city or town, the same house. Of course, once you move, you take it in stride—at least I did—but for them it was much harder because they remembered what they'd left behind. Even I divide my time between New Hampshire and New York, so I think I carry something unsettled in me, some desire to go back and forth. There are other people like that, too, so I don't know if this is just due to my background. My good friend Mark Strand is even more restless than I am. He always wants to go someplace. There are people who had no desire to leave Strafford, New Hampshire, and I understand that, but . . .

I think of Emily Dickinson, who rarely went anywhere.

One time she went to Boston—and there was Washington, too, right?—but she hated both places. She couldn't wait to get back.

Let me read you a few quotations that are going to be familiar to you. My question is: Are you sympathetic to any or all of them? This is about poetic form. Robert Creeley said, "Form is never more than the extension of content." Denise Levertov revised that to "Form is never more than the revelation of content." Your friend Charles Wright: "Form is never more than a transubstantiation of content." And Frank O'Hara: "You just go on your nerve."

I know all four of them. I like Denise Levertov's formulation the best. It makes sense to me, although it has a religious, even mystical dimension to it—the idea that form is a revelation of content. In other words, we don't choose a form of the poem, but it is revealed to us in the process of writing it. So, for example, if you're lying under a tree in the shade after lunch, a heavy summer lunch of fried chicken, corn on the cob, watermelon and much wine, you look out there and see a beautiful meadow, maybe horses, summer sky, and you feel good about the world, and maybe you have a notebook and a pen and you attempt to write about this feeling, this sense of the moment, that mood would influence how you wrote. I don't think you would write in very short lines, choppy lines. You'd sound more like Roethke than Creeley; your lines would get longer and longer. Or say you're on a farm, and your wife comes in and brings an egg that has just been laid, a brand new egg in the palm of her hand. A nice-looking egg, a perfect egg, and you feel moved to write about it. Well, it's likely to be not a long-winded poem but something more compact, pared down, careful about every word and image, not because you've decided ahead that it should be so, but because the experience itself of seeing that egg has revealed to you how to proceed.

"We don't choose a form of the poem, but it is revealed to us in the process of writing it."

You wrote once (in a letter to Charles Wright), "The ambition of each image and metaphor is to redescribe the world or, more accurately, to blaspheme." A consistent theme in your work is blasphemy—thumbing your nose at power, at convention, at institutions. Is the blasphemy of the young man, the Simic of his twenties and thirties, the same as that of the older Simic?

Sure. Poets are in competition with God. He has his idea what this is all about, and we have ours. Look at American poetry since Whitman and Dickinson; they are all constructing their little model of the universe. So, yes, I'm still at it, happily blaspheming away.

Finally, I have a multiple-choice test for you. We can go through this rapidly, then tally your responses and see how you did.

Sure.

Coleman Hawkins or Lester Young?

Lester Young.

Fellini or Bergman?

Fellini.

Howlin' Wolf or Lightnin' Hopkins?

Lightnin' Hopkins.

Schoolhouse or prison?

That's a tough one. Prison.

Dusk or twilight?

Dusk.

Rooftop or fire escape?
Rooftop.

Porcupine or armadillo?
Porcupine.

Whitman or Dickinson?
Dickinson.

Eliot or Williams?
Williams.

Frost or Stevens?
Stevens. But I love them both.

Bishop or Lowell?
Bishop.

Polka dots or stripes?
Stripes.

Congratulations. A perfect score.

Birdsong
Mom?
Can you hear me?
Mom? It's me...
Johnny?
N—no Mom, it's Paul. Dad died a long ti—
Johnny I've missed you so much!
What was it like over there in Japan?
Look, I—
Mr Byrne, you might want to play along for a little bit—it could jog her memory some. A lot of these folks don't know left from right—you're lucky she remembers as much as she does!
Oooh—K...Well, ah...Japan, Japan was...very hot. We saw many...temples. There was this beautiful mountain, and—and all the houses were made out of paper.
PAPER?!

Yes! And—ah—I was very tall there.
Were the women very beautiful?
Not as pretty as you, Peggy.
Did you miss me?
Always.
How you've AGED! That war put twenty years on you!
Well—ah...
I've been dreaming of this day for so long! It feels like an eternity since you left...
It's been so hard without you here, Johnny!
And—and—oh, Johnny!
Johnny—I never told you—I was gonna have a BABY...
But you were away so—I—I had to get rid of her, Johnny! Tell me, what else could I have done? Now that you're back, we can start a family proper, hm? You still want to marry me, don't you, Johnny? Hm?

Why're you looking at me like that? Johnny? You killed too, didn't you? You killed little babies over there in Japan, I'll bet! Didn't you then? What else was I to do?
Don't upset yourself like this—let's talk about something else—please!
You're right, you're right—I'm just so happy to see you again after so long!
We should be celebratin'! Will you dance with me, Johnny Byrne?
Wait now! Just—just sit yourself back—I—I really don't think you should be—
Nonsense! I know just the song.
N—nurse?
Now where'd I put those records?

Ah, no matter! Come dance with me, then!
You sure you're balanced OK?
Can you hear them birds singing for us? Hm?
SHUFFLE SHUFFLE
WHOOPS!!
MA!!
Mom!?
Are you OK?
C'mere Johnny
C'mere Johnny...Johnny! Oh, Johnny...you have no idea how badly I've needed you all these years!

RESCUE
what
is
good
IN
me.

Tête-à-Tête

Matthew Baker

It's not like the ice rink downtown is a private establishment for members only with plastic membership cards that get scanned at the door; it's a public rink that anyone can go to who owns a pair of skates, or even anyone who doesn't, because if you want you can rent them at a window inside, and anyway you don't even have to skate, it's totally normal just to come and order one of the concession stand's city-renowned pretzels and sit at one of the tables along the edge of the rink and just watch everyone, or play videogames at the arcade next to the bathrooms by yourself having a good time, and if my boyfriend was going to take out some bimbo with a fur jacket and her own ice skates instead of yours truly on a super romantic date where they're wearing mittens and holding hands and are more snuggling than even skating out on the ice, he could at least have had the decency to take her to a private rink, am I right? Where I'm not going to happen by the rink on that very same night of their super romantic date, just planning on getting a pretzel and maybe a soda before going out to one of the many costume parties and ballroom galas to which I'm frequently invited, and to which my boyfriend could not garner even a single invitation unless he happened to be dating yours truly, as he's not even that cute and is an economics major which is considered *très* boring among the playwrights and trombonists and escape artists with whom I tend to hang? So what am I to do, but wait until my boyfriend and the bimbo part ways, my boyfriend skating off toward the concession-stand side of the rink, the bimbo skating off toward the arcade-and-bathroom side, or, at this point, my side, as I happen to be heading toward the women's bathroom at that very moment?

In the bathroom the bimbo takes the extra large handicapped stall, despite the fact that she exhibits not even a single physical handicap, and the additional fact that all of the normal-sized stalls are also unoccupied, and when I hunch down on my knees outside of her stall, I see that she's already tugged her super ugly black jeans down around her super dumb ankles. All the better—I'd rather not do this face to face.

I knock on the door of her stall, and she says, "Someone's in here," which obviously I am already very aware of, and which I think is exactly what I should be saying to her about *my life* and *my boyfriend.* Instead I say, "That guy you're with has a girlfriend." Then, of course, from pants-around-her-ankles, the expected, "Excuse me?" I reexplain the situation: man, extant girlfriend, you're a bitch.

Then things get *très* freaky, because I hear the lock on the stall door snap open, and then pants-around-her-ankles tries to open the door—pants still around her ankles! Which, does she think I really want to see *that*? Thanks but no thanks. So now I'm holding the door shut, and she's inside trying to kick it open with her pants-around-ankles monoleg, and that's when a mom with a saggy face and a twin kid attached to each hand comes swinging through the bathroom door, looking at me like, Jesus, this goddamn city.

Inside her stall the bimbo's saying, "Prove it," and I say, "His name is Peter Inconnu and he likes cop movies and no sugar in his coffee," but then before I have a chance to present any additional compelling evidence I see through the crack in the door that pants-around-her-ankles is in the process of transforming into a fully mobile pants-pulled-up-onto-her-hips, so I run past the saggy-faced mom and her twins and out the door back into the rink proper. Then I get my coat from my table and zip it up to my chin and tug my hood over my face and decide I've suffered enough shock and humiliation and outright degradation for one night, *merci beaucoup*. But after I leave, I wait outside the front entrance of the rink, peeking in through the windows, until I've seen bimbo skate back out to my boyfriend at the center of the ice, where he's waiting for her with a cup of something warm, and from the way they start swinging their arms around, I can tell that bimbo's asking him about me, and now they're fighting, and everything is good, so good.

✯

Back at my studio I find a note from my landlord reminding me that exterminators are coming in the a.m., the necessity of which seems iffy to me, as I haven't seen a single insect or rodent or even nonhuman in my apartment since moving in a year ago, and as I am a private person who doesn't like having her apartment exhibited or her belongings trifled with, I call my landlord's office number and leave a message saying that I do ever so appreciate his offer to send a number of strangers with foul-smelling sprays to come visit my digs, but as I'm currently caring for my great-aunt, a great-aunt who's just recently been confined to bed, a bed located in this very same studio he's planning to fumigate in the morning with black-market toxins, I'll definitely have to pass.

Then I call my sister to tell her the latest about my supposed-to-be-perfect boyfriend, and of course she doesn't answer, as she's probably either mad at me or busy getting skewered by her super nice husband on one of the counters of their super expensive flat. To which I would say—mad at *me*? Whilst thou are skewered by a dreamboat husband, and thy unfortunate sister doth suffer outrage after outrage at the hands of lesser men? My sister's husband is only so nice because he's from Canada, and in Canada they don't know how to be anything but. He and my sister work at an advertising company downtown, whose job it is to make people believe that toothpaste is *so* much better than just toothpaste. She's always mad at me for things I didn't actually do. Like when we were younger and our father went off to Paris with someone we'd never met and left my sister in charge for an entire week, and the other fifth graders on my bus asked why I was riding the bus instead of our father driving us like always, and I told them that my father had gone off to Paris with someone we'd never met and had left my sister in charge for an entire week, but when my sister heard she got mad at me for being what she thought was *très* untrustworthy and jejune, because all she'd told the ninth graders was that our father was busy and couldn't drive us, because she was afraid of kidnappers and burglars and also our father who apparently had specifically said that we weren't allowed to tell anyone about how he'd left us alone for the week, or alone at least except for the credit card he'd given my sister in case we wanted to order pizza or rent movies, which even though she hadn't told the ninth graders about Paris, she'd already shown them and the fifth graders and even the bus driver *that.* My sister has also gotten mad at me for flirting with her husband who was then just her boyfriend and who was actually flirting with *me*, for wearing an orange dress to her college graduation party when I knew she was planning on wearing an orange dress except that I *didn't*, and for entirely forgetting about her twenty-ninth birthday and not sending her a present or a card or even calling her except that I was super unwell at the time and basically just throwing up and vomiting and retching and dry heaving her entire birthday weekend, and how is one supposed to put together the customary birthday tribute for one's sister when one is more or less on one's deathbed at the time of the birthday in question? Moreover, does a twenty-ninth birthday really merit that much fuss to begin with? Wouldn't one think one's sister would prefer not to commemorate her being on the brink of middle-ageness, cultural irrelevance, and the general loss of good looks?

I take down the half finished sculpture from along my windows, which I've been working on as a surprise for my boyfriend, and which I now plan on destroying, either by wrench or by hammer, or by tossing it off the roof of my building and into the street. Then I notice—this sculpture is way too genius for me to just smash apart over a boy, am I right? Future generations might never forgive me? While I'm deciding what to do with it I accidentally finish an entire bottle of wine. Then my sister calls me back. "What," she says. I can hear dumb-advertising-party noises in the background. "What what?" I say. "What-did-you-call-me-for what," she says. I tell her about how my supposed-to-be-perfect boyfriend has fallen in love with someone with superstar breasts and a cute button nose. "Since when is he a boyfriend?" she says. "Are you taking his side?" I say. "I can't believe you're taking his side." "Well," she says, "what's so good about him anyway?" "Everything!" I say. Which then I realize is true. At which point I realize that I can't destroy the sculpture, because I still want to give it to him. So I tell my sister about how the button-nose bitch took a handicapped stall and how I was about to kick in the door on her when some middle-aged woman showed up with her entire brood, at which point I realized that it wasn't the fault of button-nose anyway, and so I decided to leave the ice rink so that I might better plot my eventual and inexorable revenge. Which my sister thinks is funny, especially the part about almost kicking in the door, and finally she starts talking like she's somebody's sister instead of somebody's stranger, and tells me that if my boyfriend prefers a probably unemployed button-nose to a city-renowned painter and watercolorist and illustrator with exceptional and in-proportion breasts, my boyfriend can go get fucked, and that if button-nose thinks she's getting away with anything by dating a traitor and a cheat, she's got a thing or two coming. Then she does some freelance advertising and convinces me that life is *so* much better than it actually is.

☆

I suffer the usual discrimination at work, my manager citing disheveled hair, wrinkled clothes, and a makeupless face as evidence of what he calls poor hygiene, which really means he's just afraid that we aren't going to sell much coffee unless us baristas maintain a fuckable appearance. He doesn't care about who he hired, about who I actually am. He wants me to be someone else. "No one wants to buy pastries from someone wearing a uniform that looks like it's been used as a dishrag," he says, "and smells like spoiled milk." Then he points out some crusted paint in my hair and asks when was the last time I even showered. I explain that this very morning my apartment was invaded by exterminators, circumstances of which I was not even forewarned, which forced me to vacate the premises, *my own premises*, for a three to four hour period, a period which I would have happily invested in a general cleaning-up-of-self, if I had only had the chance. At which point, as if to quite possibly stress out yours truly to the point of complete and utter mental collapse, my boyfriend walks into the café, wearing a super cute scarf.

I duck into the back and pretend to be slicing pears. Dessek the barista peeks through the doors. "We're getting slammed," he says. I say, "Can you just cover for me a minute?" Dessek says okay, only because he's been head-over-heels in love with me since day one of my temporary employment here at this city-reviled café. Dessek's uniform is wrinkleless, and his face appears recently soaped—obviously I hate him. For a while I read a magazine someone's left in the back. Then Dessek peeks in again. "Wasn't that that guy you were dating?" he says. "I don't want to talk about it," I say, flipping a page, not even looking at him.

And anyway, if my father still bothered to pay my rent I wouldn't have to do the servile chores of a barista, but when my sister got married he cut the both of us off at once, which is why I was mad at my sister for almost an entire year. I consider my sister's marriage a tragedy that forced the both of us to grow up too soon. Our father is one of the wealthiest contractors in the city—if we had both stayed single, he probably would have kept paying our rents till we were fifty. But of course the last thing my sister cared about was whether or not I ended up on the streets—for her it was just love love love. *Très* cliché.

Which somehow she even ended up blaming *me* for—talking to her about anything is talking to her about how you aren't good enough. She's just like my father. Tell him you made some new friends, he'll say if you've got time for that, get an internship. Tell him you got a boyfriend, he'll say at your age your sister was already engaged. Tell him you learned a recipe for roast fennel and quail, he'll say last week he found a restaurant that makes the best quail in the city. If you don't make enough money to keep your apartment? Watch less television, take night classes, find a man who'll buy you your dinners.

My manager comes into the back. "What are you doing reading a magazine?" he says. "I'm on break," I say. "You got here twenty minutes ago," he says. I say, "Dessek said he didn't need me." Then I ask if I've sold any paintings since my last shift. I let the café sell my paintings—it likes to pretend it's a part-time art gallery. "No," he says. I once saw him stare at the butt of another barista for a full minute—she was bent over, picking up some pecans she'd spilled onto the floor. My friends know all about him. I'd tell his wife about him too, if she ever came into the café. But Dessek says she has mouth cancer and keeps smoking anyway even now that she's hooked up to machines, so I guess that won't be anytime soon.

I go out front, take an order for a small chai latte, make it, ring it up, then let Dessek take back over. My boyfriend is sitting over by a window, eating some sort of pastry. I guess he hasn't noticed me. "Did you two break up?" Dessek says, dolloping whipped cream onto somebody's coffee. "Jesus," I say, "it's not like we were even that serious. We only went out three times. If I decide I'm not that into him, what's the big deal?" "Oh," Dessek says, buttering somebody's toast. "I thought you were more serious than that." To which I think, don't get any ideas, Dessek the barista—a recently soaped face will only get you so far. Dessek got kicked out of college for cheating on an essay test. He wanted to be a doctor, since his family is from India, but now he just works at a café. His life's going nowhere.

"Anyway," I say, "he's already started dating someone else." Then while Dessek is washing out an empty carton of milk I tell him about how I happened to run into them at the ice rink, and how his date started talking shit to me in the bathroom—from inside her stall, no less—and how I kicked in her door on her and then left her there, pants down, door open, and laughed the whole way home. "Funny," Dessek says. He has to pretend not to like me, to cover up how googly-eyed in love with me he actually is.

Dessek has to run into the back to get more milk, so I take someone's order, and when she orders a coffee I ask, "Sweetener?"—like our manager has told us we're *supposed to do!*—and she says no thanks. After I've cashed her out, my manager comes over and says, "Don't say sweetener—that makes it sound artificial and cheap. Ask if they want agave nectar or raw honey, so they know it isn't fake." "Since when is our honey *raw*?" I say, because

I know it isn't. "Since always," he says. Of course he's itching his crotch through his pants this entire time.

☆

Back at my apartment it looks like the exterminators never ended up coming after all—apparently my landlord got the great-aunt message in time to call them off. How I know is that the exterminators came through once before, and after they left my apartment smelled like rotten lemons for an entire week. But when I get back tonight, no lemons.

I'm supposed to hang out with my friend Carlo C., but he's not answering his phone. I'm afraid this might mean he hates me again, which sometimes he does, for only the stupidest of reasons. While I'm waiting I take off all of my clothes except for my socks. Then I stand in front of my mirror. Then I stand an imaginary naked button-nose bitch next to me and compare our bodies. What I like best about myself are the dark freckles on my nose and my cheeks, the bigness and whiteness of my teeth, and my clavicles. What I like best about the imaginary button-nose next to me is the smallness of her lips, the smallness of her eyes, and the way her breasts will sag in twenty years.

Someone knocks on my door. I think: boyfriend? Although I know it can't be him, because he doesn't know where I live, unless maybe he waited outside the café and then followed me home. He almost walked me home once after one of our dates, although I didn't care that he didn't—who wants to be walked home by an uncute economics major who can't even be bothered to pay for his date's coffee? Especially yours truly, the *crème de la crème* of twenty-something women? As we were at the café where I work, it didn't really matter—Dessek never charges me for coffee anyway. But my boyfriend—or now maybe ex-boyfriend—didn't know that.

It's my landlord. Of course I put on some shorts before opening the door, and also a sweater. "Rent?" he says. "I don't think my heater's working right," I say. "And I hate being cold more than anything." "Yes, but what about the rent?" the landlord says. He has a stomach you could fit small children in, if they were curled up in the right way. "Well, I have the money, but I think I ought to save it, just to be safe, because I don't have a job anymore," I say. "No job?" he says. "What happened to your job?" "I quit," I say. "It just wasn't working out. But I have a much better job lined up anyway, and I just sold a series of large paintings, so it will all work out. I'll send you a check next week." "Did everything go okay with the exterminators?" he says. "I don't think they came," I say. "Didn't come?" he says, squinting at me and rubbing his children-carrier. I say, "Doesn't smell like they did. What were they even supposed to kill?" "Anything in the building that doesn't belong," he says. "If they weren't here today, they'll be here tomorrow." "But what about my great-aunt?" I say. "What am I supposed to do with her?" "What great-aunt?" he says. "If you've got a second person living here we'll have to renegotiate the rent." "I never said anything about anyone living here," I say. "I was just asking about my great-aunt, but never mind." "Okay then," he says. "Exterminators tomorrow."

I bid the man *adieu* and again take off my clothes. I have the heat cranked up to eighty, because I really do hate being cold. I call my father about the rent, but he of course doesn't answer, and I don't bother to leave a message. I look in my cupboards for something to eat but can't find anything except for salty things, and if I loathe anything as much as the cold, it's salt. The worst part about seeing my ex-boyfriend at the café was that even after he definitely saw me he definitely didn't even bother to come over and say hi. Which, if you had recently had an adulterous ice-skating-with-a-button-nose date cunningly ruined by someone whose identity was unknown both to you and the button-nose in question, wouldn't you want to tell the story to just about *everyone you know*? Especially a woman with adorable freckles who had not once but thrice treated you to *gratuit* coffee and the most exquisite *tête-à-tête* imaginable? A woman with unparalleled abilities in sculpting and baking and the speaking of French? But apparently, despite her smallness of lips and smallness of eyes, button-nose had charmed him to the extent that he'd forgotten my very existence.

Carlo C. calls. "Hello?" he says. "Hi," I say, and explain who I am, in case he forgot. We met once at the supermarket—Carlo C. asked for my number, then gave me his. "Oh, that's right," he says. "Sure, sure, I'll come over." Carlo C. is a renowned attorney with a firm here in town.

I put on my orange dress and mid-thigh striped stockings. Next I try and fail to clean my apartment. Next I accidentally drink an entire bottle of wine. I call my sister but she doesn't answer. I hook on hoop earrings that are *très* hip, take them off, hook them on. Carlo C. is at the door and I'm holding it open, been holding it open—how long? Not sure. I decide no more wine for at least twenty minutes.

"Sorry if there's bugs," I say. "The exterminators are coming in the morning." Carlo C. is unfazed by the prospect of being set upon by creepy-crawlies. "Cool sculpture," he says. "It's based on my ex-boyfriend," I say. "If you can't tell it's him, that's okay—it's abstract." "I like it," he says. "Very cool." Carlo C. is wearing a black button-up and smells like sex. I don't mean sexy—I mean he smells like he just had sex, very wet and sloppy sex, so recently that it almost surely must have happened somewhere in the stairwell outside of my door. "Anyway," I say, "I was going to destroy it, but if you want it, it's yours."

I tell Carlo C. we should go out to a costume party or ballroom gala but Carlo C. says he loves the ambiance in my apartment (*bien sûr!*) and wants to stay here. He opens a bottle of wine and washes one of the snifters in my sink and pours himself a drink. I turn on some electronica, which I assume Carlo C. will like, as he's from somewhere in Eastern Europe.

"Don't you work at a café here in town?" Carlo C. says. "I think I've seen you there." He's sitting on my futon, so I sit down next to him. "No, not anymore," I say. "My manager told me they couldn't afford to pay someone ten dollars an hour to come in and read magazines, or to chop up an entire box of pears that was supposed to last us the entire month. In other words, we're not allowed to take breaks—which *has* to be illegal—but we're not allowed to do extra work either. Work too little, you're fired! Work too much, you're fired! So I quit." "Too bad," Carlo C. says. "I like that place." He's playing with one of my hoop earrings. "It only happened because my ex-boyfriend came in and I got all upset," I say. "Him?" Carlo C. says, pointing at my sculpture. "Yes, him. Just last night I caught him with another woman," I say. "They were out ice skating, and from the second you saw her you could tell *exactly* what sort of woman she was—ugly fur coat, super ugly black jeans, and him already snuggling up all over her. This in front of families—with children! I was supposed to meet my friend, a city-renowned skater—" "Who?" Carlo C. interrupts. "Does he play hockey? I love hockey." "No," I say, "he *hates* hockey. He's a figure skater. Anyway, as soon as I saw my ex-boyfriend with her out on the ice, I called my ice-skating friend and told him not to come—it's totally platonic, but my ex-boyfriend was always jealous of the skater anyway, because the skater has super huge arms and a super rugged jaw and is an artist, and my ex-boyfriend was not even that cute and had girlish arms and a girlish jaw and was a mere econ major—*très* boring, am I right? Maybe now I'll date the skater, now that things are over between me and my ex. Anyway, I ran into the bathroom because I was so upset—and who do you think follows me in but my ex-boyfriend's new cunt-in-a-fur-coat? I don't know how she recognized me, but she came in saying shit like, 'Excuse me,' and 'What are *you* doing here,' and when I tried to explain that excuse *me* bitch but you happen to be out on a date with *my* boyfriend, she said, 'Prove it,' as if she'd sooner believe *him* than yours truly. At which point I was wishing I *had* let my ice-skater friend come, so I could have stood him up next to my ex-boyfriend and said to her, look, who gives a shit about your new cock-in-a-cute-scarf, because he's pale and bony and thinks *cop* movies count as favorite films." Carlo C. pours more into his snifter. "I love skating," he says. "We should go sometime." "No, I hate it," I say. "Anyway, I told her to get fucked. Then I went banging out of the bathroom. But as soon as I did, I realized I had a whole lot more to say to her, so I went banging back in. She was in one of the stalls—apparently she'd had other business to tend to in the bathroom, aside from victimizing me—the handicapped stall, no less, with someone in a wheelchair already waiting in line outside of it. So I knocked on the door and told her what I really thought of her coat and my ex-boyfriend, and told her that if she thought she was getting away with anything by dating a traitor and a cheat, she had a thing or two coming. Then she said, 'Where do you get off, thinking you're better than me, just because you've got perfect teeth and perfect freckles? You're just a lonely bitch with no real friends.' So I went to the sink, pounded on the soap dispenser about a hundred times until I had an entire handful of it, asked the woman in the wheelchair to wheel out of the way, and then kicked open the stall door, and I slapped her with my soapless hand, and then when she screamed I shoved my hand with the soap over her mouth and let her choke some of it down, really taste it. My father used to do this to us when we were younger—rinse our mouths out with soap if we said something bad." "My mother used a wooden spoon," Carlo C. says, tipping the rest of the bottle out into his snifter. "Not on our mouths, on our asses. But my brothers and I always had it coming." "Well so did this bitch," I say, "and she got it. I left her gagging down the rest of the soap. 'She's done now,' I said to the woman in the wheelchair as I walked out the door. 'It's all yours.' She gave me a thumbs up—she was on my side."

"Damn," Carlo C. says. "So what'd you do to the ex-boyfriend?" "Nothing yet," I say. "What do you think I should do?" "As an attorney, I'm not going to say anything," Carlo C. says, twisting the corkscrew into another bottle of wine. "But as Carlo, I say that soap trick is pretty funny—maybe hit him with that." "No, he'll get something a whole lot worse than that," I say. "Well, if you do anything naughty, like naughty in the illegal sense, I'll defend you pro bono," Carlo C. says. "I'll only do something I can get away with," I say. "Well, if you want pro bono, I'm yours," Carlo C. says. "The past couple months I've been defending a murderer—it'd be a nice change of pace." I kiss Carlo C. We kiss for a while. Then we take a break and drink more wine. "I mean I don't really give a shit about him or anyone," I say, "but still it hurts to get passed up for someone else. Even if she's not better, it makes you think she must be." I swing my legs up onto the futon. "Who?" Carlo C. says. I kiss him again. "You have nice hair," he says. Then we kiss again, for so long that I'm not sure if we've ever been not kissing or will ever be not kissing ever again. Carlo C. kisses my cheekbones and my eyebrows and my forehead and my cheeks, and he says, "You deserve someone better," and I say, "I know," and he says, "I'll take good care of you," and I keep kissing Carlo C., but as I'm doing it, I know how my ex-boyfriend must have felt when he was holding that bimbo's hand through their mittens—how you can touch someone, and be thinking of someone else the entire time—I kiss Carlo C.'s dimples, and I'm thinking of the tiny gap between my ex-boyfriend's teeth, and Carlo C. kisses my shoulders and I unbutton his button-up, and I'm thinking of the way my ex-boyfriend used to stir his coffee with a spoon even though he never took any milk or sugar, no sweetener, no agave nectar or honey, raw or otherwise, and Carlo C. shoves my dress up over my hips and spits into his hand and makes what isn't wet wet, and I touch Carlo C.'s ears and his jaw, and the more I touch them the more I love the way my ex-boyfriend could talk to a complete stranger about economics and not be embarrassed or shy about loving such a nerdy nerdy thing, back when I was a complete stranger, when we first met, and as I tongue Carlo C.'s tongue the more of Carlo C. that I taste the more it makes me forget him, and I think, is this how my ex-boyfriend felt, holding the hand of that button-nose, but thinking only of me? And what now, now that I know this, know how he truly felt? When I have sent Carlo C. away again, will I have any choice but to gather my shoes and my half-finished sculpture, and to trek through the night, by subway or by bus, to the apartment of my boyfriend, to end this silly quarrel? To tell him he's forgiven? To tell him that my love is a love that will not be beaten? To tell him that I want nothing more than to buy drapes with him, and eat ice-rink pretzels, and read books to him under the covers of a bed we'll someday buy? How else could it ever have happened? I will buzz his door, and run up his stairs, and when he sees me he will be so happy—*très* happy—so happy now to not be alone.

I Keep My Kidney Stones in a Salt Shaker

John Allen Taylor

On the top shelf of my book case
between a guide on egg identification
and my grandfather's red Darby Bible.
A friend told me it's like a smoker keeping
cancer in a box of Winstons. I don't have any
idea what that would look like, but it sounds
nothing like the intricate, calcified
crystals my kidneys turn out from time to time.
Snowflakes cast in stone, the color of raw
sugar, each one a different, unique pain.
They clink in the shaker when I bring
it down to make a deposit. I never look
at them, but I know they're beautiful, coral-
like, tempered and porous like an ostrich egg.
Sometimes I wonder if Jesus
ever had kidney stones, if his doctor
recommended drinking a six-pack in a warm tub.
I wonder if that centurion's spear tore through
years of scar tissue—if Jesus said to Thomas,
"This is where they were."
But the old Darby has nothing on Jesus' kidneys.
I think if he had kidney stones he would keep them

in a salt shaker on his top shelf between
a six-pack of Fat Tire and his grandfather's
copy of Song of Songs.

(the result is constellation)

Kristen Orser

A universal rejection out of the tube,
a sudden explosion:

An invitation

to stick flowers between my ribs,

and embroider a wingtip. The country shifts, promptly obtains a new sense of place. Do we fall behind head and accelerate the question or discover a corner to put our bodies, all questions.

The bones in our bodies *and how they get out of order.*

(like bees round their hive)

Kristen Orser

Looking like the devil,
a little pine tree suggests

Pluck your body
from the orchard.

Wheelbarrow in a long direction and remind yourself that this pretty noise on the roof is difficult to understand.

The gigantic danger of breathing
is the interruption

of how we come to exist, become long in the face, and arrive with flowers
under the fruit tree—entirely insane. I want to say furiously,

I slept the whole night like a duplicate, but my lubricated heart is definitively hollow
(howl?).

GOD
LOVES
the
MEEK

Going Native

Caitlin McGuire

Tammy was tired of theory and wanted to sleep with an Indian. A card-carrying, reservation-born Native American with a drinking problem and a ninth-grade education. Since Michael had decided that long distance wouldn't work out, the thought had become the focus of nightly episodes in which she swayed in the center of Ponderosa's pine-paneled bar to the ghost of Hank Williams and Patsy Cline. She imagined being interrupted by a warrior, like Uncas from *Last of the Mohicans* or Abel from *House Made of Dawn*. They'd drink too much, the way they drank in the movies. He'd take her home; she'd let him think it was his idea. She wanted to be conquered and needed a warrior, which is why she found herself in Strychnine.

The bar was less full of lonesome cowboys than she had hoped, and pulsed instead to dub-stepped beat; the floor was gummy and clung to the prick-points of her heels; nothing was at all like the bar of her imagination, where she had two-stepped barefoot. She'd read that Strychnine was an Indian bar, but her one-sixteenth-Cherokee, diluted by Chinese and Irish blood, seemed to carry the red man demographic. Granted, she was only six miles from home, but she'd expected Strychnine to feel like another dimension. She felt cheated by *The Toughest Indian in the World* and Seattle, a city covered with Salish salmon designs but no Indian as far as the eye could see. She sidled up to the bar.

"I'll have a whiskey, neat." Tammy had never had a whiskey, neat or otherwise, but she wanted the courage of the old west.

The bartender set the glass on a coaster in front of her. Tammy adjusted her short, brown dress and slid onto a stool at the edge of the bar and cradled the drink between her hands. She wanted to make a ceremony out of the first taste. Her tongue—the whiskey—molasses, smoke, and Christmas. Whiskey tasted like hard Southern living.

The man on the barstool next to her swayed standing up, his arm with its Rainier clutched haphazardly, jostling onto her legs without apology. The stories they told during freshman orientation about girls who drank alone never ended well. But that was the point, wasn't it? She took a drink, and her stomach lit up, warm with the 90 proof. Didn't she want to do something risky? She had written pages upon pages about Indians for her senior thesis; didn't she deserve to touch one? To escape the pages of her books and make her writing real? The more she drank the easier it was to drink more. She stared through the whiskey at the coaster underneath: Kokopelli, magnified by glass. She tipped the rest into her mouth, closing her eyes, and when she finished she looked across the bar. An Indian looked back at her.

"Her tongue—the whiskey—molasses, smoke, and Christmas."

He waved two fingers, not to call her over, but in recognition, a salute that said *you exist and I have seen you.* His hair was just as black as hers, though longer and braided. He seemed authentic. She bit her lip and glanced at the wall, flushed, and suddenly very aware that she had only slept with one man in her life. She rolled the empty glass back and forth.

Tammy didn't know anything about seduction, but she did know that she was tired of reading about beautiful red people doing beautiful purple things in beautiful green places, and she wanted something beautiful for herself, so she smiled at him. He patted the man next to him on the back and whispered in his ear, then held up two fingers to the bartender and pointed at Tammy. The bartender set down two glasses of whiskey in front of her, each uncomfortably full. They left a wet path behind when she pulled them closer.

The Indian stood next to her. "I'll trade you."

"Trade me?"

"A glass for a name."

"Tammy."

He held his hand out, offering her a drink. On closer inspection, he was handsome in a way her boyfriends had never been, without the fragility of Sean's Anglo-Saxon cheekbones and the freckles that dotted his shoulders, without the smoothness of Jun's skin, without Michael's bristly, black stubble from the beard she begged him to shave. He was strange angles, of rough noses, and full lips, *the bold outline of his high, haughty features.* He took a drink and grimaced. "Fuck, you drink firewater." She laughed. He looked young, recently off the rez. He had a green shirt on, frayed at the seams, the black outline of a tree on the front and Sequoia National Park written underneath. "Don't you want to ask my name?"

Tammy looked him over. Odds were, his name would only disappoint her. She didn't want him to have an average name. She wanted him to be The Man With The Turquoise Stone Heart. She wanted him to be The Man With Scars On His Back. She wanted him to be The Man Who Would Paint Rivers Over The Hollows Of Her Hips With His Braid. She wanted him to be The Man Most Likely To Take Her Home. "I don't want to know yet."

He drank from the glass, and Tammy watched the corners of his mouth twitch. "So what are you going to call me?"

She squinted. "Geronimo."

"Geronimo." He rolled the name over in his mouth, considering it. "I like it." He smiled a dogtooth smile.

"So, Geronimo, how do you afford your firewater?"

He pushed back into the bar stool next to hers. "I'm a third year at UW. You?"

"Fourth year. What are you studying?"

"Statistics."

Tammy shook her head. She wanted him to be passing through: a priest, a poet, a heart full of something more than numbers.

"Don't like statistics?"

"Not much," she said. Tammy believed in right arguments, not right answers. "I wasn't really any good at math."

"Statistics isn't just math. I mean, there's math, but there's more, too. We get to interpret the math. Numbers are just numbers without a context."

Tammy didn't know how to flirt over math, or the context of math, so she gripped the glass in front of her, and when she lifted it, the alcohol dripped down the sides. She leaned forward to keep her dress dry. "Give me an example?" The whiskey burned.

"I don't have the numbers to back me up, but I'd say that you sitting alone at a bar is statistically unlikely."

She laughed. "Who said I'm here alone?" She thought he blushed, but it was hard to tell.

"I saw you come in. What are you studying?"

"Ethnic studies. I'm turning in my thesis on Native Americans tomorrow."

"Native Americans—cool. I grew up next to the Barona rez in San Diego." Not on the rez, then, but near it. "Native Americans in general, or something more specific?"

"Depictions of sexuality, actually."

He raised his eyebrows. "I don't know if I'm allowed to say anything now."

"Are you a Puritan, Geronimo?" Her eyelashes felt heavy.

"Far from it." He pinched the collar of his t-shirt. "But you know, the things you don't talk about with new people—sex, politics, religion."

"I think those rules only apply if you plan on having long-lasting friendships with the new people."

His eyebrows twitched. Tammy looked at him, the boy with the darkest skin in the crowd, so brown-red-russet it revved her courage and made her think of beautiful things she wanted to do to him. Wispy hair at the nape of his neck had come out of his braid, and he seemed momentarily breakable. She wanted to feel the braid on her neck as he pulled his face close to hers. She had spent years studying things she didn't understand, couldn't understand, couldn't touch. She wanted context. She wanted to touch him. She wanted him to be The Man Who Made Things Make Sense For A Night.

> "Tammy didn't know how to flirt over math, or the context of math, so she gripped the glass in front of her."

She picked the glass up and finished it, ignored the burn, swallowed hard. She put it upside down on Kokopelli. "You're here alone, too?"

He motioned across the bar. "Well, I'm here with friends, but not *with* anybody."

"How do you feel about being plus one?"

He downed his whiskey. "I think I feel alright about that."

☆

Geronimo lived in a dorm with posters of Che and Crazy Horse on the wall behind his desk and books full of math on his shelves. The room was spartan, clean for a boy, or at least cleaner than the rooms of most boys she'd known. Michael's had been a mess. No bedframe, an aura of books around his mattress; they had spent a year on the floor. No possibility of that, not in the room with a twin bed against the wall.

She leaned back against the short hallway where the door swung into the dark room and looked at him, her hands pressed hard behind the small of her back, pushing on her hipbones. Geronimo leaned against the bedframe like they'd known each other for more than an hour in a bar and a bus, like he'd already touched her the way she'd been wishing, *touch my shoulder, touch my cheek, kiss me, because I am lost and afraid.*

She bit the inside of her mouth and pulled one hand out from behind her, smoothing her hair behind one ear. It had gotten a little wet during the walk to campus. He was so dark. She wanted him to touch her first. It was windy outside and the building groaned, burying itself into its foundation. The mist had left a spider web on his hair. Why wouldn't he touch her?

"Do you," he cleared his throat, "want to watch a movie or something?"

"Not particularly."

She blinked. Why did her parents ever warn her about men and sex? They never seemed to want sex, or at least they never seemed to want her, they never seemed like they understood anything at all. She always led the breadcrumb trail to her body. In her romantic history, she'd never fended off advances; never been thrown up against a wall in brutal passion; never been wanted so much they couldn't make it home. Maybe modern men were lazy. She didn't want modern men. She wanted the warrior. She put her hand back behind her, and he scanned the room for another distraction. She rolled her eyes and wondered if she'd picked the wrong Indian. Maybe this one was too young. Maybe he didn't know what to do with a woman. He was a year younger than she. Just one year. Was it possible that he didn't know what it meant when a woman asked to be brought home? When she pressed her hips out, did he not know that he was to pull them close to his, to take the breath out of her throat? She had never struggled to have her body language understood before, but maybe Michael had a translation guide Geronimo couldn't touch.

"So what do you want to do?"

She looked up at him, but didn't answer him; didn't want to have to be in charge; wanted the warrior. Maybe this was a mistake. She licked her lips, and he made eye contact with her, and she hoped that her hazy eyes looked beautiful and sober and promising. The wind blew harder and the floor moved under her feet. Whiskey was stronger than she had expected. She felt brave but didn't want to make the first move. He leaned back into the wooden bedpost, and she thought about statistics, and science, and the way the words the body used had nothing to do with the words their mouths did. Why wouldn't he touch her?

He pushed off the bedframe and walked across the room, standing on the opposite side of the tiny hallway, but still, he didn't touch her. Her confidence, thin at best, faltered; maybe she wasn't enough. Maybe she didn't know the body language that meant *I want you for tonight, then become a memory.*

"Why don't you want to know my name?"

"I know your name. You're Geronimo."

"My real name. Why don't you want to know my real name?"

"Because it's better this way." She inhaled, her chest rising as anxiety took hold, and she exhaled hard to push it out again.

"What if my name is ridiculous?"

"Then I'll be surprised."

"Do you want to hear it?"

"No."

"What would you do if I told you my name?"

"I'd leave."

He took a step forward, got as close as he could possibly get without touching her, and she breathed in. Exhaling would mean they'd have to touch. She wasn't sure anymore. This had felt easy in her head, but the body that was so close to her felt threatening in ways her imagination had never been, and she didn't want to bridge the gap; she wanted to deflect, run down the hall, and exhale without another body so close. She really should have been working on her thesis. She thought about the end of *The Last of the Mohicans*. She hated the movie, its thousand digressions from the original. But the way Magua held out his hand. The silence. Alice jumping off the cliff. That wasn't the way the book ended.

> "Maybe she didn't know the body language that meant *I want you for tonight, then become a memory.*"

"Would you leave now?"

The inches fell apart, her face moved toward his, and he was gentle. He kissed too softly, with more wetness than she usually liked, but it wasn't unpleasant. She pressed her hips toward him; he didn't press back. He pulled her hand to wrap around his waist and made her meet him. Geronimo kissed her again, and she touched the braid, a thrill rushing through her spine, finally.

He was tender, and as she pushed him and moved to make him move, she realized that she was fighting a losing battle. He wasn't The Man Who Makes Love Like The House Is On Fire or The Man Who Thrusted Until He Was Done or The Man Who Ravished White Women. He was The Boy Who Met A Girl In A Bar, The Boy Who Worried About Women's Feelings, The Boy Who Brushed Women's Hair Off Their Faces And Kissed

Their Eyelids. She worried that she had judged him too quickly, that this was a mistake. But as mistakes went, it was a pretty good one.

☆

Tammy pulled the elastic band from the end of his braid, wiggled her fingers in between the strands, and slowly pulled the twists apart. His hair was crimped by the plait and the rain that had dried shiny in his hair.

Geronimo sat up, and his legs danged off the side of the bed. He slid on his boxers, and as he leaned forward, the waterfall of hair reached halfway down his back. She ran her finger down his spine and counted vertebrae. She felt like sex itself, lying on top of Geronimo's yellow sheets, and she pointed the tips of her toes out to touch the wooden footboard.

He stretched his neck, rolling his head from side to side, and stopped to look back at her. "So, do you have a last name?"

"Chen."

"Really? You don't look like a Chen."

"My dad's a Chen. My mom's an O'Brien."

"That makes more sense."

"What are you?"

He crossed the room and filled a glass of water at the sink. "Animal, vegetable, mineral?"

"You know what I mean. Like, ethnic, tribal."

He leaned back against the sink as he drank. "Does it matter?"

"No, not really. I'm just wondering." She laid back into the bed, pressing into the thin mattress.

"I'm American. But my parents are from Mexico." She opened her eyes.

"Thirsty?"

"No," she said too quickly. She reached for the sheet and wrapped herself tight. She groped for her dress on the floor, and he handed it to her, then turned to face the opposite wall. It was sweet, the privacy he gave her as she dressed, but it was something else as well. She pulled the dress up, but the zipper was caught on the fabric.

He turned and watched her fight with the metal teeth. "Need a hand?"

"I've got it." She didn't.

She felt his hands on her skin, cold from the glass of water still, and he leaned down to look at the zipper more closely, his nose grazing her waist. He teased out the fabric that obstructed the teeth.

She stared straight ahead. "What's your name, Geronimo?"

"Carlos."

"Are your parents Aztec, Carlos?"

"I don't think they call themselves that anymore."

She looked down at him on his knees. "But are they?"

"Maybe my parents' parents' parents' were."

"That's a native right? And Mexico is part of North America, right?" She swallowed and let her eyes grow wide. "Does that make you a Native American?"

Carlos put his hands on his knees, pressed up to his feet. Tammy hadn't realized how tall he was in the bar when they were sitting down, but now, she appreciated the tall reed of him, the slimness and the lean muscles that moved with his twisting. "Did you think I was an Indian?"

She looked away.

He laughed. "When's that thesis due?"

"I should go."

He looked at the clock on his nightstand. "It's three in the morning. You're welcome to spend the night, if you want."

"No, I should go." Tammy slipped her feet back into the too-tall heels she had worn earlier in the night. The wind had died outside, and the room was unearthly in its quiet.

"Do you want me to walk you home?" He began braiding his hair again.

She grabbed her purse from the foot of the bed. "No, I'm fine. I don't live too far from here."

"She stood in the tiny hallway again. She was uncomfortable with being uncomfortable; how do you say goodbye to someone you only briefly met after they've been inside you?"

"If you're sure."

She stood in the tiny hallway again. She was uncomfortable with being uncomfortable; how do you say goodbye to someone you only briefly met after they've been inside you?

"Well."

"Well."

Tammy pressed forward on her tiptoes and kissed him on the cheek. She left alone.

As she walked the ten blocks back to her apartment, Tammy listened to the sounds of parties on the Ave and looked away when she passed the Burke Museum. No more Salish salmon. The semester was coming to a close, and in five hours, she would be dropping off her thesis with her major adviser; three months, and she'd be starting grad school. Ethnic literature. She rubbed her forehead with her hand. She wished she could tear her thesis apart and start again.

When she got home, she opened her laptop and hit print. She didn't want to read what she'd written, and she didn't care about what she had thought. As the printer cartridge ran back and forth, echoing in the hollow darkness, she stripped for the second time that night and climbed under the covers on the left side of her bed. She still hadn't learned to sleep in the middle.

Tammy didn't know what to think of before she fell asleep anymore. Patsy Cline didn't comfort her, nor did James Fenimore Cooper, definitely not sex. She wasn't The Woman Who Strung Together Twenty-Thirty-Forty-Fifty Pages Of Bright Thoughts. She wasn't The Woman Who Brought The Text Into Her Flesh. She wasn't The Woman Who Seduced An Indian In A Bar.

Native American In A Bar, she corrected herself. Native American.

On Heroism & the Oregon Trail

Kit Frick

We like to think we are secret beauties. To think we are big ships. We like to think we are noticed, in secret, by some keen eye, and it is enough. It is never enough.

Remember the Oregon Trail? How our Conestoga wagon made it through cholera, through the South Pass, through snakebite and starvation until winter outmatched us? We were not the winning team. Never enough.

We like to think we are small-town heroes, but what small town would claim us? We are the heroes of this poem only. This poem will not draw back the curtain to reveal an ordinary man at the helm or our true beauty. This poem will not bestow upon us prize money or a new life out west. At its end, we will say good morning to our failure. We will say, indeed we died, but how the west was fun!

Promise us this: don't forget us. Oh, please don't turn this page. That would be the wrong kind of ending. That would sincerely break us.

Afternoon Sex

Graham Murtaugh

The unexpected connection
unloading groceries. The purple eggplant
molded perfectly to your hand. I bend
to close the dishwasher and turn
into you. A mimic dance, a moment
where we roam, dip into cups and pockets
before the call goes out: *all hands report!*
Move to the bedroom, quickly shuck shirts
and jeans and socks and tangled bra
all helter-skelter, dive under covers.
The mail slot bangs. The neighbors
with the yapping dogs chat just beyond
the window. We keep quiet, cram
our greedy mouths full of the other's tongue,
grip the handholds God so knowingly provided
and hang on. We riot in silence.
Quick as a summer shower it passes, trailing
a sparkling curtain and the scent of wet pavement.
We collapse, spent, sleeping the incautious sleep
of unlooked-for victory.

A Very Personal Reflection on My Lesson about *Lord of the Flies*

Nicholas YB Wong

Pedophiles also love plants.
Mimosa, for example. Or anything that

folds like the skin around the dimples
of these kids. Their flesh so clean, so free
from the trauma of hugs. Rain

pours outside, I think of pineapples

& how my face looks like one.
Instructions: Who said these lines (& in

what context would you say them to me)?
This head is for the beast
It's a gift / You're not wanted
The world . . . slipping away / maybe it's only us /
I painted my face now you eat
and I—

Pages are turned like the body of
a cheap whore, casually but with

expectation. The kids bury their heads
between lines, between thighs, to look for
a remedy for adulthood. How one loses one's

head just by growing up.

Blanks in worksheets are bald heads (incl.
mine). Fill them with

hairs.   (yours)

I play a film clip in which a conch
breaks. Calcium is symbolic in its

                                shattering:
you all escape, upon the bell, for vanilla
scoops & I, scopophilic in class with goose
-bumps on my arm honking. Certain

taboos require a table & a book to sound dirty.

[After we felled the Noble fir]

Jennifer Moore

After we felled the Noble fir, you washed the sap from my hands. In the sink, the soap and the sap and a nest, a bed of needles. You read my future in their pattern: *You'll do this, you'll do that. It will be this way.* True, all of this happened: a pair of hands in the mirror, a gathering of dark matter. We traced the lines of pine in the white basin and left the tree outside, a cut thing.

We axed the tree and left it overnight. In the morning, its branches were traced with the evening's weather, each needle made clear by the frost that encased it. In this way I can approach any past: shake the snow from the limbs, bring the body inside.

Somewhere farther north, elk wander into the next season and pine needles bend to wind, collecting along the banks of the river. A different kind of departure: a man who locks eyes with a woman in a mirror and will not look away, or the movement through town of a hearse with no body inside.

come
home.

ILLUSTRATIONS BY KELLY CLANCY

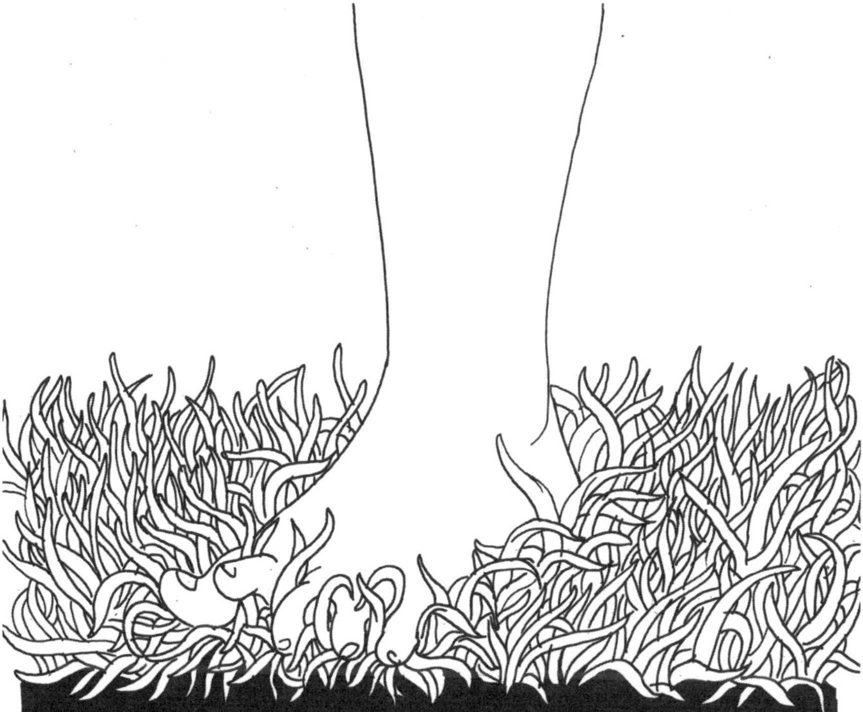

Artist's Statement

I work with ink, paper and words. I'm interested in memories, and how they fit together to compose the stories we construct our identities out of. I strive to make collaborative art, such that the narratives that come out of my comics disclose as much information about the mind of the viewer as they do about my own.

—Kelly Clancy

Contributors

Kim Addonizio is the author, most recently, of *Lucifer at the Starlite: Poems* and *Ordinary Genius: A Guide for the Poet Within*, both from W.W. Norton. Her collection of stories, *The Palace of Illusions*, is forthcoming from Counterpoint/Soft Skull in 2014. She teaches writing workshops at her home in Oakland, California, and online. Visit her at www.kimaddonizio.com.

Matthew Baker's stories have appeared in *American Short Fiction*, *New England Review*, *The Missouri Review*, *The Kenyon Review*, and *Best Of The Net*, among others. He is the primary translator for the interlinked novel *The Numberless*, the randomized novella *Kaleidoscope*, and the intentionally posthumous *Afterthought*. He lives in Ireland.

Matt Bell's debut novel *In the House upon the Dirt between the Lake and the Woods* will be published by Soho Press in June 2013. He is also the author of *Cataclysm Baby*, a novella, and *How They Were Found*, a collection of fiction. He teaches creative writing at Northern Michigan University.

Mark Jay Brewin Jr. won the 2012 Agha Shahid Ali Poetry Prize of the University of Utah Press for his first book manuscript, *Scrap Iron*. His poems have been published or are forthcoming in *Southern Poetry Review*, *New Madrid*, *The Hollins Critic*, *Copper Nickel*, *Southern Humanities Review*, *Poet Lore*, *North American Review*, *Greensboro Review*, *Prairie Schooner*, and elsewhere. He is a graduate of the MFA program of Southern Illinois University-Carbondale.

Kelly Clancy studied physics at MIT, then worked as an itinerant astronomer for several years. After serving with the Peace Corps in Turkmenistan, she published a graphic memoir about the war in Central Asia, written from the perspective of women and children affected by America's war on terror. She is now a National Science Fellow at Berkeley and hopes to unlock the secrets of the brain by shooting lasers at it.

Liz N. Clift holds an MFA in Creative Writing from Iowa State University. Her fiction appears or is forthcoming in *qarrtsiluni*, *Tulane Review*, *Green Mountains Review*, and others. She lives in the American West.

Kevin Cyr was born in 1976 in Edmundston, New Brunswick, Canada. He grew up in Madawaska, Maine, and received a BFA from Massachusetts College of Art in Boston. Cyr is currently based in New York. His paintings, drawings, sculptures, and installations have been exhibited by galleries and museums internationally. Over the years he's developed a body of work depicting run-down vehicles covered in rust, dents, and graffiti as a way to talk about the changing landscape of America. He has also been focused on creating large-scale sculptural pieces that expand his interest in vehicles to incorporate shelter.

Chris Forhan is the author of three books of poetry: *Black Leapt In*, winner of the Barrow Street Press Poetry Prize; *The Actual Moon, The Actual Stars*, winner of the Morse Poetry Prize and a Washington State Book Award; and *Forgive Us Our Happiness*, winner of the Bakeless Prize. He is also the author of two chapbooks, *x* and *Crumbs of Bread*, and his poems have appeared in *Poetry*, *Paris Review*, *Ploughshares*, *New England Review*, *Parnassus*, and other magazines, as well as in *The Best American Poetry*. He lives with his wife, the poet Alessandra Lynch, and their two sons, Milo and Oliver, in Indianapolis, where he is associate professor of English at Butler University.

Kit Frick is the author of *Echo, Echo, Light* (winner of the Slope Editions Chapbook Contest, forthcoming in 2013). Her poems have recently appeared in places like *DIAGRAM*, *Conduit*, *CutBank*, *Sixth Finch*, and *Forklift, Ohio*, and have been featured on Verse Daily. A 2012 "Discovery"/*Boston Review* semi-finalist, Kit is the chapbook editor for Black Lawrence Press. Kit lives in Brooklyn with her husband and lives online at www.kitfrick.com.

Sarah Heffner holds degrees from the University of Pittsburgh and NYU, where she also taught creative writing. Her poems have appeared in *The North American Review* and *The Three Rivers Review*. She lives in South Korea.

Pam Houston is the author of five books of fiction and nonfiction, including *Contents May Have Shifted*, *Cowboys Are My Weakness*, and *Waltzing the Cat*. Her stories have been anthologized widely, including in the *O Henry Prize* volumes, *Best American Short Stories*, and the *Best American Short Stories of the Century*. She teaches creative writing at UC Davis and Pacific University and lives at 9,000 feet in Colorado near the headwaters of the Rio Grande.

Andrew Hudgins teaches at The Ohio State University. His most recent book is *American Rendering: New and Selected Poems*. In 2013, he will publish two books: *A Clown at Midnight*, a book of poems, with Houghton Mifflin Harcourt, and *The Joker*, a memoir about being a compulsive joke teller, with Simon and Schuster.

Douglas Light won the 2010 AWP Grace Paley Prize for short fiction for his collection *Girls in Trouble*. His novel *East Fifth Bliss* was adapted into a film starring Michael C. Hall, Peter Fonda, and Lucy Liu. His second novel, *Where Night Stops*, received a 2012 NoMAA Grant.

Micah Ling lives in Brooklyn and teaches in the English department at Fordham University in Manhattan. Her third collection of poetry, *Settlement*, was released by sunnyoutside press (Buffalo, New York) in 2012.

Lee Martin is the author of the novels *The Bright Forever*, a finalist for the 2006 Pulitzer Prize in Fiction; *Break the Skin; River of Heaven*; and *Quakertown*. He has also published three memoirs, *From Our House, Turning Bones*, and *Such a Life*, and a short story collection, *The Least You Need To Know*. He teaches in the MFA program at The Ohio State University.

Michael Martone was born in Fort Wayne, Indiana. Now, 57 years later, he lives in Tuscaloosa, Alabama, where he teaches writing at the university there. He writes himself as well, mostly about himself, Indiana, and being born there, and about writing and writing about writing.

Caitlin McGuire is a James Dickey fellow at the University of South Carolina and co-founded *Cartagena Journal*. Born in California, she's still not clear on where the West ends.

Teresa Milbrodt is the author of the short story collection *Bearded Women: Stories* (Chizine Publications) and the upcoming novel *The Patron Saint of Unattractive People* (Boxfire Press), which will be published this fall. Her flash fiction collection, *Larissa's Guide to Trying to Be a Good Person in the World* (Pressgang), will be published in the spring of 2014. Milbrodt's stories have appeared in numerous literary journals, and several have been nominated for a Pushcart Prize. She lives in Gunnison, Colorado, with her husband, Tristan, and cat, Aspen. You can read more of her work at her website, www.teresamilbrodt.com.

Jenni Moody holds an MFA from the University of Alaska Fairbanks and is a graduate of the Clarion West Writers Workshop. She's lived in a dry cabin in Alaska and a small town in Japan and was once chased by a family of bears through the Yukon at midnight. She collects stamps (inked, not licked) and writes in the company of her partner and her two black cats in Huntsville, Alabama. Her website is jennimoody.com.

Jennifer Moore has poetry published or forthcoming in *American Letters & Commentary*, *Barrow Street*, *Best New Poets*, *The Volta*, and elsewhere, and criticism in *Jacket2* and *The Offending Adam*. She holds degrees from the University of Colorado and the University of Illinois at Chicago, and teaches creative writing, composition, and literature at Ohio Northern University.

Graham Murtaugh is a poet, writing-workshop facilitator, and civic-engagement wonk. He lives and writes in Portland, Oregon. More of his work can be seen online at grahammurtaugh.com.

Josh Neufeld is a comics journalist known for his graphic narratives of political and social upheaval, told through the voices of witnesses. He is the writer/artist of the bestselling nonfiction graphic novel *A.D.: New Orleans After the Deluge* (Pantheon). In addition, he is the illustrator of the bestseller *The Influencing Machine: Brooke Gladstone on the Media* (W.W. Norton). He was a 2013 Knight-Wallace fellow in journalism at the University of Michigan. www.JoshComix.com.

Chris Offutt grew up in Haldeman, Kentucky. He is the author of *Kentucky Straight*, *Out of the Woods*, *The Same River Twice*, *No Heroes*, and *The Good Brother*. He has published more than seventy stories and essays, including appearances in *The New York Times*, *Esquire*, and GQ. He has received awards from the Guggenheim Foundation, the Whiting Foundation, the Lannan Foundation, the NEA, and the American Academy of Arts and Letters. He wrote screenplays for *True Blood*, *Weeds*, and *Treme*, and TV pilots for Fox, Lions Gate, and CBS. He lives in Oxford, Mississippi.

Kristen Orser is the author of *Winter, Another Wall* (blossombones); *Folded Into Your Midwestern Thunderstorm* (Greying Ghost Press); *Wilted Things* (Scantily Clad Press); *Squint* (Dancing Girl Press); and *E AT I*, illustrated by James Thomas Stevens (Wyrd Tree Press). She is recently the recipient of SLAB's Elizabeth R. Curry Prize in Poetry. She lives near the Pacific but misses Lake Michigan.

Summer Pierre is an illustrator and writer and the author of *The Artist in the Office: How to Survive and Thrive Seven Days a Week* (Perigee Trade). Her work has appeared in numerous places, including *Slice Magazine*, *Loaded Bicycle*, *The Huffington Post*, and a zine she creates called *Forgive Me*. She lives in the Hudson Valley with her family.

Katharine Rauk is the author of the chapbook *Basil* (Black Lawrence Press). She has poems published in *Harvard Review*, *Georgetown Review*, *Paper Darts*, and elsewhere, and she is an assistant editor of *Rowboat: Poetry in Translation*. Her poems have been choreographed by dancers as part of Sandbox Theatre's word/move project as well as performed by the musicians of the Willamette Jazz Collective. She lives in Minneapolis and teaches at North Hennepin Community College.

Suzanne Richardson earned her MFA from the University of New Mexico in 2012. She currently lives in Utica, New York, where she is an assistant professor of English at Utica College. Her work has appeared in *New Ohio*

Review, *New Haven Review*, *Blood Orange Review*, and *Front Porch*, among others. You can find more of her work at www-suzannerichardsonwrites.tumblr.com.

David Ryan's fiction has appeared or is forthcoming in *Fence*, *Hayden's Ferry Review*, *The Encyclopedia Project*, *failbetter*, *Unsaid*, *BOMB*, *Tin House*, *Denver Quarterly*, *Alaska Quarterly Review*, *New Orleans Review*, several *Mississippi Review* Prize issues, *Nerve*, *Cimarron Review*, *Salt Hill*, and *Hobart*, among others. His work has been anthologized in *Flash Fiction Forward* (WW Norton), *The Mississippi Review: 30*, and *Boston Noir 2: The Classics* (Akashic).

Porter Shreve is the author of three novels, all published by Houghton Mifflin Harcourt: *The Obituary Writer*, *Drives Like a Dream*, and *When the White House Was Ours*. He directs the Creative Writing Program at Purdue University.

Chris Speckman earned his MFA from Butler University. His work is forthcoming in *PANK* and *Word Riot*.

John Allen Taylor is a knower of small things. Among those things are goldfishes, California poppies, and 1940s glassware. He lives in the Pacific Northwest and is at this moment sprouting lentils.

Claire Vaye Watkins was born and raised in the Mojave Desert. Her stories have appeared in *Granta*, *One Story*, *The Paris Review*, and elsewhere. Her story collection, *Battleborn*, won a Silver Pen Award from the Nevada Writers Hall of Fame and inclusion on the National Book Foundation's "5 Under 35." An assistant professor at Bucknell University, Claire is also the co-director of the Mojave School, a nonprofit creative writing workshop for teenagers in rural Nevada.

Charles Harper Webb's latest book, *What Things Are Made Of*, was published by the University of Pittsburgh Press in 2013. Recipient of grants from the Whiting and Guggenheim foundations, Webb teaches in the MFA Program in Creative Writing at California State University, Long Beach.

Scott William Woods writes from the Connecticut shoreline. His short fiction has appeared in *The MacGuffin*, *The Blotter*, and *Black Fox*, among others. www.scottwilliamwoods.com.

Nicholas YB Wong received his MFA at the City University of Hong Kong and is a finalist for the *New Letters* Poetry Award. His second poetry collection is forthcoming from Kaya Press in fall 2014. Corgis are his favorite human breed.

GREETINGS from
INDIANAPOLIS
INDIANA